# ORANGE BERETS

## Adventures and Misadventures
## In the Sinai

## by
## James "Doc" Crabtree

This book is dedicated to the MFO peacekeepers, particularly to those who lost their lives while serving in the interests of peace.

I would also like to acknowledge the role my wife played in getting this book put together. She insisted that I do something with all those cartoons I keep drawing and hopefully they will now bring a smile to a few faces. Finally, would also like to thank the following former members of the MFO for their help in putting this new book together:

Jeroen Scheffer, Peter Benicsak, Ross McClure, Rich Millbank, Maria Pia Herrera Starkweather, April Robb, Andy Allen, and Danita Nolen.

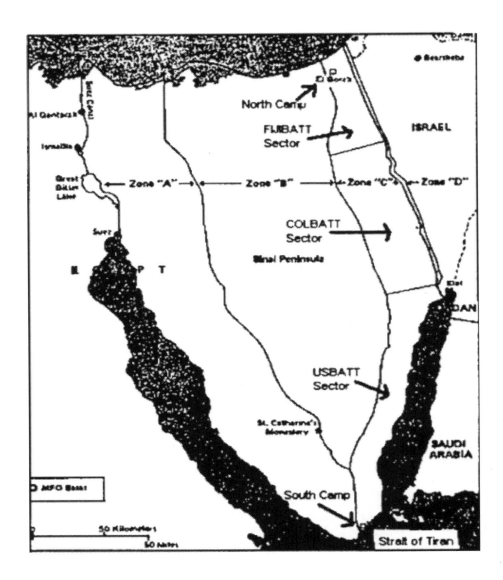

# TABLE OF CONTENTS

# Jimmy Sinai Books

## Fayetteville, NC

First Edition: 2015

Titles by James D. Crabtree

*On Air Defense*
*Guerrilla Air Defense*
*Orange Berets*
*Desert Fox 1998*
*Guerrilla Air Defense II*
*Secrets and Scuds*

# INTRODUCTION

The Sinai is the crossroads of history. From time immemorial there have been migrations, invasions, expeditions and marches across its sands. Throughout history the Sinai has served as a bridge between two continents and its vast wastes have served as a border between nations, cultures and religions.

It all started when mankind's earliest ancestors wandered away from the lush Nile valley to the west of the peninsula. Once they reached the other side of the Sinai desert early humans wandered north to Europe or further east towards what would become Persia, India, China and even the Polynesians and early Americans.

With the rise of civilization the Egyptian pharaohs established the greatest kingdom ever seen up to that time, with an enduring religion, a written language and monumental art. However, they met their match in the Hyksos, who invaded from the east around 1700 B.C. and moved into the Nile Delta. Their chariots, the tanks of the day, rolled along the Mediterranean coast of the Sinai, the shortest and easiest route across this unforgiving land and the favorite road of invaders ever since.

The Egyptians sorted out the Hyksos and reunited Egypt into an even more powerful kingdom. In an effort to protect their eastern boundaries the Egyptians crossed the Sinai a hundred years later and started conquering the "Asiatics" they found on the eastern side. Their own use of chariots made this task easier.

Babylonians came next, conquering the Asiatic states that Egypt controlled in Palestine. Nebuchadnezzar II briefly invaded Egypt in 567 BC via the Sinai but must have had second thoughts when he saw the supply problems involved. He settled for leaving the Sinai as a border frontier. Besides, Babylon had troubles of their own with the Persians.

In 525 BC it was the turn of the Persians to cross west through the Sinai and conquer Egypt. Cyrus the Great's army, which was composed of over 120,000 troops, had soldiers clothed in color-coded uniforms, an ancient first.

Alexander the Great was no slouch when it came to conquests. Starting out in Macedonia, he conquered Greece and employed a variety of units in combined arms operations. By the time Alexander marched west through the Sinai he had units of Cretan archers, Greek hoplites, Thracian cavalry and a host of other military specialists crossing the desert to install a Greek dynasty that would last until Cleopatra's time.

Egypt was in the midst of a Civil War in 48 BC between Cleopatra (actually, Cleopatra VII) and her brother Ptolemy XIII, with Julius Caesar caught in the middle with about 4,000 Roman soldiers in Alexandria. Caesar had come up with the idea of peacekeeping but found out that neither side was interested in peace. He prudently asked for help and Mithridates of Pergamon marched west through the Sinai to help his Roman ally.

When the dust of history cleared, Rome was no longer a republic and Egypt was one of Imperial Rome's provinces. The Sinai became part of another Roman province, that of Arabia Petraea. If Roman legions did not march through the Sinai during the power struggle between Octavian and Mark Anthony they certainly did so when things got out of hand in Judea. During the First Jewish-Roman War the XV Legion marched out of Alexandria and headed east through the Sinai to put down Jewish rebels.

A new Persian Empire used the Sinai to invade Egypt next, around 618 AD. The Persians invaded Egypt because it was vital to Byzantium, to which it now belonged because of the Fall of Rome.

The Persians did not hold on to Egypt long, when it was reconquered by the Byzantine Empire. Next came the turn of Islamic Arab armies who crossed the Sinai after crossing conquering other Byzantine territories to the east.

Crusaders crossed the Sinai from the Kingdom of Jerusalem in the 1160s in an effort to support one Muslim ruler over another in the Caliphate that ruled Egypt. This would not prevent the Muslims from eliminating the crusader kingdoms once they got their respective acts together in Damascus and Cairo.

The Ottomans came next, in 1517 AD. For the first time artillery pieces were trundled west along with the invaders. The Ottomans defeated the Mamluks who ruled Egypt at the time and it became a part of the Ottoman Empire.

Napoleon Bonaparte next arrived on the scene, in 1798. After becoming France's most successful general, while at the same time becoming a very dangerous political figure, Napoleon was given the mission of taking Egypt and then possibly moving eastward to threaten the British, who would remain France's number one enemy over the next couple of decades. He succeeded in taking most of Egypt and then proceeded east through the Sinai... in the direction of India. Napoleon got as far Acre (in present-day Israel) before retreating back across the Sinai, with the Ottomans following at a leisurely pace.

Egypt became semi-independent of the Ottomans under the rule of Muhammad Ali, a Muslim Albanian general sent by the Sultan to restore order. Later Egypt would be semi-independent under the British, which would still be its status when World War One broke out. A Turkish force, led by German generals, crossed the Sinai in 1916 to attack the Suez Canal, a strategic piece of property on the western side of the peninsula, but had to settle for occupying a few towns and villages. The Central Powers used aircraft to support their operations.

The Allies (mostly British and Australians) crossed the Sinai in 1917. They had airplanes and armored cars as well as cavalry.

In 1948 Egyptian forces crossed the borders of what used to be Mandatory Palestine to squash the Israeli war of Independence. The Egyptians had British tanks left over from WWII.

In 1957 Israeli forces crossed the Sinai westward to link up with French and British paratroopers who seized the Suez Canal. The Israelis were supported by first-rate French-made Jet aircraft. Israel occupied the entire Sinai Peninsula but had to give it back.

In 1967 Egyptian forces massed in the Sinai in order to strike at Israel in conjunction with forces in Jordan and Syria. Following preemptive airstrikes the Egyptians retreated all the way to the Suez Canal. The war ended with Israel in control of the Sinai. This time they did *not* give it back.

In 1973 The Egyptians, striking at the same time as the Syrians, crossed the Suez Canal and began moving through the Sinai under the protection of an "umbrella" of surface-to-air missile systems provided by the USSR. The Israelis persevered and crossed the canal, destroying the missile sites and opening up ground forces to air attack once again. Israel remained in control of the Sinai.

The United States assisted Israel with weapons and spare parts. The USSR equipped the Egyptians. The situation was getting out of hand now that the nuclear powers were involved. Something had to be done or the Battle of Armageddon might indeed take place...

# CONUS REPLACEMENT CENTER 1

I arrived at the Continental United States Replacement Center at Fort Benning, Georgia in February 2007. It was the first time I had ever been to this particular post, which was mostly concerned with training Infantrymen: paratroopers, mechanized infantry, light infantry, you name it. If your job involves walking to the objective, riding to it or jumping on it then you go through Benning. Since I was a former Air Defender there didn't seem to be a need before for me to go to the Infantry theme park before.

By that time I had an interesting career: I started out as an enlisted soldier, won an active-duty ROTC scholarship, got commissioned and sent to Operation Desert Storm and Desert Shield. I had a break in service during which I went back to Ohio and was settling down to a life of academia... until I was called back to the U.S. Army.

At this time I was a major with a recent tour in Iraq behind me. While I didn't consider myself an expert on the Middle East by any means it *was* an area of study for me and I certainly had enough time in Saudi Arabia, Kuwait, and Qatar to at least be comfortable in the environment. At least as comfortable as one can be when there are rockets occasionally being fired at your Baghdad base or the *mutaween* watching you in Riyadh to make sure you're not wearing an offensive Aladdin t-shirt (There's no point in explaining the difference between a *Djinn* and Robin Williams to the Religious Police unless you want some very strange looks and a whack with a small stick).

Recently I received orders to report as the new Press and Visits Officer (SOPV) for the Multinational Force and Observers, the peacekeeping force in the Sinai. I had heard of the MFO but never met anyone who had served in it before. I only knew what I read on websites, and like that famous online quote from Lincoln says "If it is on the internet then it must be true."

The CONUS Replacement Center, or CRC, is a facility for sending individual soldiers overseas to serve in a variety of roles. The vast majority of troops deploying to Afghanistan and Iraq depart as units, so the unit as a whole goes through briefings, training, weapons qualification, inoculations, briefings (I know I put "briefings" down twice, but the Army really LIKES briefings), medical exams and administrative paperwork together, usually at

NEW ASSIGNMENT

their home base. Individuals sent as replacements, or to fill new personnel requirements identified after units depart, go through the same process at the CRC and then are provided transportation overseas via Atlanta.

Somehow along the way my gear missed my connecting flight to Columbus, Georgia, the closest town to Fort Benning. Or maybe it was left behind to ensure that the puddle-jumper we flew on would be able to get off the ground. Even without my duffelbags I was afraid that the extra book in my carryon might make our tiny plane little tail-heavy. But the misplacement of my gear was OK, because the next day the Army very conscientiously provided me with a lot of *new* desert gear... in addition to the things I already planned to bring. When my bags finally showed up from the flight (no doubt brought in on a leased crop duster) I realized I had three full duffelbags to take with me on my commercial flight overseas. Three HEAVY bags.

We were assigned to companies as part of the Replacement Battalion. We were only supposed to be at the CRC for 96 hours, and then we would be shipped off. This is probably one of those Army rules designed to prevent soldiers from being stuck in this Georgian corner of Limbo. We had personnel going to Kosovo, Djibouti, Qatar, Ethiopia, Egypt, Iraq, Afghanistan, and so on and so on, reading like a list of the 25 Most Dangerous Places on Earth. Up to 30,000 personnel went through the CRC in any given year when both Iraq and Afghanistan were going strong.

However, much of the CRC training had a "one size fits all" feeling to it. Some of the training involved recognizing and responding to IEDs, or how to put a tourniquet on yourself, or one of many other items familiar to anyone who has already done OIF or OEF or both.

My group of replacements immediately went into briefings and presentations. I sat through a cultural awareness briefing on Iraq because no cultural awareness brief was available on Egypt. Army logic states that you MUST have a cultural brief before you depart for your assignment and since they speak Arabic in both Egypt and Iraq the culture must be the same... right?

It could have been worse. We might have gotten a cultural brief on East Timor instead. After all, East Timor is very close to Egypt when you list the countries alphabetically so they must be a lot alike... right?

The medical screening was something else again. We were given vaccinations, including a booster I received for anthrax. Any other shots I can take but every time I get a jab of the anthrax vaccine I have a different reaction to it: once it was a knot the size of a cherry, another time a sting that lasted for a short time, another it was a burning that only kicked in a few minutes after the shot and lasted 30 minutes. In this instance it just made me a little queasy and for much of the remaining time I was at Fort Benning I felt sick.

# THE ADVENTURE BEGINS

They had us show up at the hospital to do our hearing tests. I suppose they had us there at 0400 so we wouldn't interfere with the processing of infantry soldiers at the facility.

I was half asleep in a sound-proof booth, trying to make out whether or not I could hear beeps on my headphone. Every time I heard one (or thought I heard one) I pressed the button.

Afterwards we sat in a waiting area and a technician came out with pieces of paper for each of us. "Here are your test results, go ahead and get on the bus."

I waited for mine but the technician looked at the name on my uniform, compared it to a sheet on his clipboard, and said slowly and loudly "SIR, THERE'S SOMETHING WE DON'T UNDERSTAND ABOUT YOUR TEST RESULTS. WE'LL NEED YOU TO GO THROUGH AGAIN."

"I'm not deaf, Specialist." I told him.

He looked at the clipboard and then looked me in the eyes again so I could watch his lips move. "ACCORDING TO THIS YOU ARE."

I did the test again and despite some high-frequency hearing loss resulting from Desert Storm I did well enough to get a medical clearance. On the other hand, I didn't have any problems with my eyes... the Army had nicely corrected my vision with lasers after I came back from Iraq and now I didn't need glasses except to read.

We went through "tactical refreshers." The last time I low-crawled or high-crawled was as a cadet in ROTC. We also went through an obstacle course and trained to do reflexive fire. I got through the pistol range with no trouble, except for a couple of jams. It probably had something to do with low-crawling while I had the weapon holstered. Afterwards I wondered to myself, exactly how much low-crawling do peacekeepers do?

When most people think of peacekeepers at all they think of *UN* peacekeepers. These are the Blue Berets, the soldiers provided by disinterested countries to some hot spot or another in order to prevent war or at least preserve the armed *status quo*. Where the Sinai was concerned, the Blue Berets had been given several chances to keep the peace and had failed each time.

The United Nations Truce Supervision Organization (UNTSO) was organized in 1948 to organize a cease-fire agreement between the Jewish population of Palestine and their Arab neighbors. This effort failed spectacularly, with the neighboring Arab states invading Palestine the very next day and the Jewish Agency declaring the independent state of Israel. There was no truce to supervise at first and tragically several members of UNTSO were killed trying to organize one. Only after Israel defeated all of the neighboring countries invading

FIRST, THE PAPERWORK

Israel were there cease fire agreements between the Israelis and their Arab neighbors.

UNTSO has small numbers of peacekeepers, rather than the larger peacekeeping forces which try to physically separate or closely monitor potential combatants. This organization has remained in place ever since 1948, watching one side or another violating the truces in place and then working out solutions by talking to both sides. This comes down to one-on-one negotiations, which worked really well in the Sinai... except for 1956, 1967 and 1973. UNTSO still works in tandem with UN peacekeepers in Lebanon and the Golan Heights but NOT in the Sinai.

The first United Nations Emergency Force oversaw to the 1956 withdrawal of the Israelis from the Sinai following its rather rapid defeat of the Egyptians during the Suez Crisis (in conjunction with the British and French occupation of the Canal Zone). Once the Israeli evacuation of the Sinai was complete the peacekeepers deployed several thousand observers along the Israeli-Egyptian border, including Gaza.

Egypt sabotaged UNEF I shortly before hostilities broke out in 1967 by demanding the withdrawal of the force's Canadian contingent, which provided the logistical support to the entire force (including aviation transport). They also ousted the Yugoslavians manning posts in Sharm el Sheikh, guarding the entrance to the Gulf of Aqaba. Before the shooting even started Egypt declared a blockade of the Gulf, cutting off Israel's only access to the Red Sea. The peacekeepers suddenly found themselves in the way of the next round of war between Egypt and Israel. When the shooting DID start many of the peacekeepers died when they were caught in the crossfire between the two belligerents.

Following the 1967 War (which is also known as the Six-Day War) and another Egyptian defeat the Israelis didn't feel much like handing the Sinai over again, since it took considerable effort to recapture it and relying on UN peacekeepers didn't really work out that well for them the last time. The Israelis figured the best way to defend Israel was to do it from the east bank of the Suez Canal.

The Egyptians rather disliked this attitude and in 1973 launched another war, gaining a foothold back into the Sinai thanks to excellent planning, new weapons and better performance by its soldiers. Egyptian troops crossed the Canal under the protection of a surface-to-air missile "umbrella," but eventually the Israelis gained the upper hand and actually pushed westward over the Canal and trapped many Egyptian troops.

UNEF II was implemented in the aftermath of this conflict, known variously as the October War, the Ramadan War and the Yom Kippur War. Since

NEXT, THE EVALUATION

the Israelis remained firmly in control of the Sinai the UN peacekeepers were restricted to the area around the Suez Canal; later they were allowed to cover the rest of the peninsula. The UN authority for UNEF II was renewed periodically but ran out for good in 1979. Many UN peacekeepers died during incidents related to UNEF II's efforts.

By this time everyone realized that a different kind of peacekeeping force, perhaps one separated from the politics of the UN, might be more effective.

Personally, I have nothing against UN peacekeepers. I was almost one myself. There I was, the Executive Officer of USADACENFB HQ Battery, checking message traffic at the communications center at Fort Bliss one day in 1993.

The first two of the three messages were totally routine. The third, however, requested that we send someone from the post qualified on the ROWPU system to Somalia. At the time, we had U.S. soldiers there as part of the United Nations Operation in Somalia (UNOSOM).

I read through the description while I was waiting for the rest of the traffic. "Oh, they're looking for someone to do reverse-osmosis water purification," I said out loud.

The sergeant looked up. "You know about that, lieutenant?"

"Well, I saw it demonstrated when I was at Advanced Camp at Fort Lewis a few years ago and why-are-you-writing-my-name-down?"

The soldier was making a note with my info on it. "Sir, you're the closest thing we've got to an expert so far in water purification."

"I didn't say I knew how to DO it... I only saw the Engineers working the big machine and asked a few questions about it!"

"Sir, we have to send SOMEBODY."

I made it my job to find someone else more qualified to go. In the interests of international peace.

Everyone in our company began departing the CONUS Replacement Center... except for me and my fellow would-be peacekeepers. A sergeant-major stopped by and explained that the holdup was in our passports... we were required to have *official* passports to travel to the Sinai, with the appropriate visas and so on. Until it was sorted out we were stuck. So much for that 96 Hour Rule.

Since we were stuck at Benning anyway we got to see the Infantry Museum, go the PX, we even looked at the jump towers where prospective paratroopers got their first taste of descending by parachute. These giant towers lift would-be paratroopers 250 feet by their parachutes and then let go. I also made a few phone calls to my wife and made some notes. Meanwhile, new

FINALLY, THE TRAINING

soldiers came in for processing. At least I shook off the effects of the vaccination and finally got some sleep after they shipped out my snoring roommate.

The day finally arrived: we were handed our brand-new official maroon passports with brand-new visas and boarded a bus in civilian clothes to take us to the international airport in Atlanta. Getting checked in was difficult, thanks to the extra gear we were all saddled with. Just moving three big, heavy duffels was a royal pain... and if we were supposed to be traveling incognito it also effectively blew our cover, what with the big "U.S. Army" stenciled on the olive-green bags.

We had a non-stop Boeing 777 flight ahead of us, 11 hours to get to Tel Aviv. We all ate and then waited at the gate.

It's interesting some of the things you see when you're just waiting around for a plane. A group of young people were also waiting for the flight, and they were wearing the gaudiest cowboy hats I have ever seen. These things had brims that were twice the width of a regular cowboy hat and were covered in either fur or plush carpeting. One was blue, one was hot pink, and I think one was a leopard pattern... I'm not entirely sure because my eyes may have stopped working for a few moments. Remarkably, the guy at security at the boarding ramp didn't bat an eye when he saw these things.

I guess in some social circles in Israel pimp hats are considered "cool."

The flight was long but uneventful. We arrived at Ben Gurion International Airport in the afternoon. The first thing that strikes you, especially if you've traveled to other places in the Middle East, is how modern and orderly everything is. Everyone also seems to be pretty upbeat. I saw a few people in uniform as we made our way to immigration control, but I didn't get the impression of a country under siege.

Finally we had our passports marked with an Israeli rubber stamp and collected our gear and we were out of the Security Zone. There were folks waiting for passengers off the planes, holding up signs and looking for faces. There were joyful reunions. There was circle dancing. There were songs being sung. There were even a couple of people taking pictures and probably getting us in the shot.... some very tired and confused Americans.

"Confused" because there wasn't anybody for US. And that's when I realized that there was no Plan B, as in "what to do if no one is at the airport when you arrive." And as the senior officer it was my job to take over and try to fix things. I spent two hours learning how to work the phone, calling the contact numbers on our orders and speaking to people over at the U.S. Embassy. The Embassy talked to the Tel Aviv MFO Office, who called the Force HQ in the Sinai. Finally I got someone on the phone who told me our flight was two hours early and that someone would be coming to collect us from the MFO.

# THE TOWER.

Two U.S. Army NCOs in civilian clothes showed up and collected us a short time later. We loaded our gear up into a van and headed for our beachfront hotel. It was quite a change from what I was used to: I had been deployed in Operations Desert Shield, Desert Storm and Desert Fox... I always did wonder why the Army never sends us to the beach. Now I would get to go to one, if only for a short time.

The hotel was first class and dinner consisted of a very good buffet. Afterwards, I wandered around Tel Aviv and walked along the beach, watching the waves coming off the Mediterranean. It looked as if all the tourist places were closed for the season, but the gift shop had lots of Holy Land souvenirs. Not as tacky as during the Crusades (with genuine I *HEART* Richard the Lionhearted pilgrim badges) but today's Holy Water magnets and olive wood Jerusalem crosses ("check out our website... we ship world-wide!") have nothing on the medieval peddlers of the religious trade.

I got a few hours' sleep but jet lag was killing me. Finally, I got up about 0300 and wandered some more.

The city was quiet and I looked at some of the memorial plaques and monuments, including the Ha'aretz Monument dedicated to the memory of the immigrants smuggled to Palestine after WWII. I passed near the U.S. Embassy, which is understandably built like a fortress. Nearby was a pub which had a sign that said "Peacekeepers Welcome." I also walked along the beach and saw some stray kittens scrounging for food.

Finally the breakfast buffet opened and most of our group was there to eat. I guess everyone was suffering from jet lag. I was minding my own business, eating my frosted flakes, when I heard an indignant female voice loudly say "what do you MEAN you don't have no bacon?!" The sergeant who flew with me to Tel Aviv further asked for (no, demanded!) pork sausage.

Obviously, the CRC needs to do some very basic cultural awareness training for peacekeepers on their way through Israel as well as the Iraqi brief. Of course, if there is no Israel brief available they might give a brief on Italy. After all, they both start with "I." That's Army logic.

We loaded up our van and headed towards Be'ersheva enroute to the Egyptian border. Along the way we passed an old Roman aqueduct, new housing developments, orchards, signs for kibbutzim and tels and Arab villages. Israel was without a doubt the nicest Middle Eastern country I have been to.

Be'ersheva was a rest stop for us and we went to McDonald's, of course. This involved going through a metal detector and being eyeballed by a security guard wearing a McDonald's shirt. I vaguely remembered Be'ersheva from Bible Study as a kid in Charleston SC, although I think my teacher pronounced it "BEAR-sheeba." Be'ersheva was also the site of a WWI battle

## NOT QUITE RIGHT

which saw the British forces take the vital town and its wells after a deception plan tricked the Germans and the Turks into looking the other way.

Once we were done eating we hopped back in the van and proceeded the rest of the way to the border. It got drier as we traveled along the way and the greenery got scarce until it disappeared altogether. The area wasn't as nice as the land of orchards and historic landmarks we had already passed. We began passing military facilities and camels.

Once at the border we were held up for three hours on the Egyptian side of the crossing. Something about our papers not being in order. I felt like it was the 1980s and I was waiting to cross the border into East Berlin. While we were waiting for the Assistant Deputy of Non-Commercial Travel to show up with his precious rubber stamp I noticed trash on the Egyptian side of the fence, stopped from going further into Israel. It gave me the impression that the trash was *straining* to get into Israel.

Finally, whatever the bureaucratic delay was it got resolved and we were permitted to proceed into the Sinai. Once we were clear of the border we drove a route which brought us near the southern corner of the Gaza Strip, marked by a formidable wall. A Fijian-manned MFO outpost was nearby and they waved at us. We then traveled along the desert roads. In the distance we could see what looked like dying palm trees and half-finished houses.

A few miles out we were told to don body armor "as a precaution." Body armor? Why would peacekeepers need body armor?

North Camp, located near El Gorah, has an Egyptian border security gate about 100 yards from the front gate of the camp, although I was never sure if it was to keep an eye on us or to keep out the riff-raff. Then we drove through the MFO gate. The camp forms one big square next to a pair of long runways.

North Camp used to be Eitam Air Base and belonged to the Israeli Air Force before the Sinai was returned to Egyptian control.

I soon found myself meeting the other staff officers. Everyone seemed pretty happy to see me... which should have made me leery. But soon after the introductions I was brought over to my room in a house that I shared with two other U.S. Army officers, the Force Surgeon and the chief communications officer.

All I needed to do now was get settled in and wait for my unaccompanied baggage to arrive.

KEEPING IN TOUCH

# ARRIVAL IN THE SINAI 2

I woke up before 0500, still suffering from jet lag. I went running around North Camp a bit.

The camp is actually very nice. The officers' housing is obviously a family area left over from the old air base and the houses (three to a billet) are pretty comfortable, each with its own shared living room, bathroom and kitchen. Three-story barracks, dining facility, headquarters, theater and other administrative building are also permanent structures. Support buildings and enlisted billets (other than the Fijian and Colombian barracks) are in trailers or other prefab buildings. On my run I also found an area near the HQ which includes the Puny Pyramids of Gorah... not to be confused with the Great Pyramids of Giza. It was probably the result of some practical joke by the Engineers. The tallest stood as high as my waist.

While water is at a premium there is still greenery. What look like hedges are actually some kind of leafy vegetation which sits a few inches above the surface of long mounds. There trees in a few strategic spots. One area, called the "forest" or the "park," is a small square of trees and plants kept alive by "recovered water." It's nice to walk through if you don't mind the occasional whiff of urine.

Outside the fence there is desert. Not a desert made of vast sand dunes, not a desert dominated by tall cacti and mesas but just flat barren earth and scrub. In my time in the Army I have somehow become a connoisseur of deserts.

I started to get in-processed with the U.S. Contingent, now officially known as Task Force Sinai. Each contributing country has a contingent that is responsible for taking care of their own personnel while they are in the Sinai. This only makes sense, as an American wouldn't know what annual training a Uruguayan has to do, or a Kiwi wouldn't be authorized to administer a written exam to a Hungarian. There were at the time 11 contingents: Australia, Canada, Colombia, Fiji, France, Hungary, Italy, New Zealand, Norway, United States and Uruguay. Each contingent has responsibilities to the Multinational Force as a whole.

After my initial collection of paperwork (to ensure I received mail, was being paid for family separation and was receiving professional "credit" for being overseas) I also had a photo taken for my Egyptian ID card. I was told that this process effectively makes one a "temporary citizen" of the Arab Republic of Egypt. I wondered out loud if this meant I could vote in Egyptian elections but then I remembered that Mubarak's Egypt doesn't really DO elections.

We were next issued our orange berets. Each contingent, regardless of what their national uniform is, wears the beret as its headgear. Officers wear an enameled white-and-orange badge portraying a stylized dove of peace with an olive branch in its beak; enlisted wear an embroidered version. The emblem also appears on the MFO's orange flags and on the white peacekeeper vehicles. I was supposed to get MFO shoulder patches too but those weren't available from Supply.

I checked on my unaccompanied baggage but the clerks at the Task Force office told me not to worry... I'd get my stuff in a couple of weeks, a month tops.

With my new patches and my introduction to the staff I was ready to get to work. Or at least I thought I was.

The SOPV office has three functions: facilitating media access to the Sinai and making press statements (which virtually never happens), providing command information to the Force (in the way of radio and TV rebroadcasts and a bilingual, bimonthly magazine) and facilitating visits to the MFO and Sinai. The Visits part of the job actually consumed most of our effort... we were like Gilligan's Island in that we were in the middle of nowhere but always had SOMEONE showing up at our doorstep.

Media access was entirely passive and rigorously controlled. No one, not MFO HQ in Rome, not the Israelis and certainly not the Egyptians want a lot of publicity. The reasons all boiled to the fact that all three parties have a good thing going and don't want to ruin it. Israeli doesn't have to station thousands of troops on its border with the Sinai. Egypt's economy benefits from having a trading partner to the east rather than a potential adversary. And the MFO HQ knows that the less publicity there is about the MFO the less likely groups in either country will find fault with their respective terms of the Treaty.

The Cairo Press Office has the last word when it comes to reporters entering and leaving the Sinai, which the Egyptian government considers a very sensitive area. During my tenure National Geographic made it known that they would like to include MFO peacekeepers in a photo article they were shooting. Now keep in mind, NatGeo already had permission to be in the Sinai and were only asking additional authorization to take photos of the peacekeepers and maybe an isolated post or two. This turned out to be impossible, despite many emails back and forth between myself and the CPO. To this day I don't know what the harm would have been to take a few pictures of Americans manning

**NEW JOB**

guard towers in southern Sinai... unless it was just that we were taking jobs that Egyptians wouldn't do.

Command Information, on the other hand, could not be left on autopilot as we did the Press portion. The previous SOPV had left without a replacement several months before. As a result the Sandpaper, the official MFO magazine, had suffered from only having one U.S. Army NCO to write articles, provide photographs, and do layout. Normally this scope of work would be done by a U.S. Army Public Affairs Detachment consisting of eight trained soldiers and a captain. The MFO architecture didn't provide for this nor was it likely we would get a PAD what with public affairs requirements for Iraq and Afghanistan competing for resources. We did get a Colombian soldier to assist us, since the magazine was supposed to be in Spanish and English.

The TV system for North Camp was very simple: it was a very low power retransmission of a satellite feed. A VERY low power retransmission. The signal was supposed to be just strong enough to be picked up by television sets on the camp but not by neighboring Arab communities, who had extremely conservative ideas about what should be on TV.

The problem was that North Camp is square and a TV transmission goes out in a circle. In order to make sure that the entire camp has access to the signal there is naturally going to be a little bit of "bleedover," especially in the center of the fence lines.

I was told that a Bedouin sheikh lodged a complaint once that if he went to the fence line with a portable, battery-powered television set and attached it to a 6-foot antenna and sat near the gate he could actually pick up I Dream of Genie and TV shows featuring unveiled women from our TV station! In order to placate him the SOPV eased back on the power for a while.

While there might be complaints about MFO-TV there were never local issues with al-Aqsa TV broadcasts coming out of Gaza. Some of these featured a bizarre Mickey Mouse-like character exhorting children to go kill Jews with an AK-47.

The MFO once had a nightly TV News program but that went to the wayside for some reason. Maybe someone accidentally reported that Mubarak had appointed himself dictator again. I thought that was too bad as it deprived the Force of a good, almost immediate source of information. The spot where the news desk used to be still had a giant photo of the pyramids for use as the anchorman's background.

The radio was entirely automated for random music content, except for a few live broadcasts by the one U.S. soldier who styled himself as a DJ. He was also in high demand as an emcee for various events.

# NORTH CAMP
# ANTENNA FARM

# REALITY ON THE BORDER

On occasion, we might be required by either the Force Commander or the Director-General to provide still photos of certain topics of interest or videotape special events. This led to an interesting episode in which we tried to video the Force Change of Command Ceremony.

We had no available videographer or working camera, so I was told to contract it. Having had some experience with contractors I wanted a test run: the videographer would first shoot an upcoming medals parade, to demonstrate his proficiency and capability. We would pay the contractor $20 for the completed (i.e., edited) test product. Then, if they did a good job, we would authorize the rest of the contract, which was $60 or so. This is a lot of money in this part of the world.

A company was found in Rafha to do the job. We asked for the identification of the cameraman who was to shoot the video. They provided a Palestinian Authority Passport and, if I remember correctly, said it was up to the MFO to get the paperwork done allowing him to cross the border. We told them to try again, since we are not in the immigration business. They sent an Egyptian citizen this time.

Medal parades in the MFO are a way of recognizing peacekeepers for their service in the Sinai prior to their departure. Each peacekeeper is authorized the MFO Medal, an international decoration, and the medal is further decorated with a numeral for each six-month period spent in the desert. I believe the group we assigned the videographer to was the Colombians.

The videographer arrived, the event was held, and the cameraman shot the ceremony. I later watched the finished video in my office. The picture had bursts of static, was frequently out of focus and the cameraman had no feel for the job. It was clear that ZERO effort had gone into the product. "What is this? A drunken monkey could have shot better video than this."

Lt. Sutherland grimaced. "The camera was really old. I got the impression that the guy they sent didn't know much about operating it."

"Well they're not getting the rest of the contract!" I said angrily. "Why would they blow the rest of the money?"

Sutherland laughed. "He has your $20. He probably paid this guy $5 and kept the rest."

"But he's out $60."

"Nope. He's ahead $15."

I had yet to learn the economics of doing business in the Sinai.

To run the visits function I was given the staff of a Canadian lieutenant (Janan Sutherland initially), a Canadian corporal and a Fijian sergeant. There was a long list of people who could visit us: MFO members reporting for the first time, family members of peacekeepers, entertainers, diplomatic personnel of the contingent countries, high-level politicians, various military dignitaries and local Egyptian and Israeli officials meeting to sort out issues of interest to both Treaty signatories. All of these visits required authorization not just to enter Egypt (if they weren't there already) but SPECIFICALLY to visit the Sinai. Coordination had to be done with the MFO HQ in Rome and the MFO offices in Tel Aviv and Cairo.

Further coordination was needed in order to provide lodging and meals while the visitors stayed at either North Camp or South Camp... we had some limited facilities for people to stay *gratis*.

Soon I was in the full swing of the meeting schedule, attending the daily 0800 brief to the Force Commander, who at the time was Major General Roberto Martinelli of Italy. His office was at the Force HQ and the FC flag flew above the building when he was present: A white flag with the MFO emblem in the center and two gold stars. I was already tending to the schedule of upcoming "bilats" and "trilats" as well as a finance meeting which will take place with civilian staff from Cairo, Tel Aviv and Rome.

It wasn't long before I learned about one of the hazards of my job: U.S. Army Central. ARCENT, as it is known, is responsible for (almost) all U.S. Army operations in the Middle East... which map-wise includes Egypt. I was soon notified that CENTCOM would be sending a Force Protection Assistance Team (FPAT) scheduled to visit the Sinai in order to assess what our security measures are for our troops and what further special procedures and equipment might improve our defense against possible terrorist attacks.

The team waited until the visit was a week out before applying for State Department clearance to visit the Sinai... and four of those days effectively constituted a long holiday weekend in the States. First I got tentative approval from MFO HQ in Rome but they didn't realize how late the request had been made. Later I got an email from our office in Cairo saying approval was NOT granted. A lot of running around but we were able to get it sorted out the following day.

Then when the team flew in from Kuwait they showed up with weapons, which made the Egyptians very, very unhappy. So unhappy, in fact, they threatened first to arrest those people who got off the airplane with weapons, then suggested they might be satisfied to simply impound the weapons and ammunition the U.S. soldiers brought with them. Unfortunately, my experience with ARCENT was that they believed they could simply go in and out of the Sinai without asking permission first. This was only the first of several problems I would have with our neighbors in the Arabian Gulf.

I was soon oriented to the mission of the MFO as a whole. The Multinational Force and Observers came about as a result of the Egyptian-Israeli

BILAT.

Treaty of Peace, or as it is normally referred to by peacekeepers, the Treaty. This treaty, negotiated under the auspices of the United States, paved the way for the withdrawal of Israeli forces from the Sinai and the return of the peninsula to the control of Egyptian authority. However, it protected Israeli security interests as well.

The Sinai was divided up into four zones: A, B, C and D. Zone A is the area east of the Suez Canal and the Egyptian Army is permitted to keep 22,000 troops in this zone along with their mechanized infantry equipment. To the east of Zone A is Zone B, in which the Egyptians are permitted to station four border security battalions, lightly armed troops who are there to maintain order.

Zone C has NO Egyptian military forces, only members of the Border Guard Force. Zone C is where the MFO is based and operates, watching key intersections and the Israeli border, which forms the zone's easternmost limit, and the land area adjacent to the Gulf of Aqaba. Finally, Zone Delta is on the eastern side of the Egyptian-Israeli border, and the IDF is permitted to keep four infantry battalions there.

The MFO forces in Zone C consist of three battalions of troops: one Fijian, one Colombian, and one American. These troops rotated into remote sites, which are observation posts placed at strategic points in the three sectors manned by each of the three battalions.

What if an OP sees something suspicious, like a couple of tanks or a column of soldiers? The OP notifies the MFO HQ of the event, providing as much detail as possible. The MFO then notifies both the Egyptians and the Israelis of what they saw and the two sides talk to each other to figure out what is going on.

The Italian Navy peacekeepers patrol the Gulf of Aqaba in specialized patrol ships, effectively making them moving observation posts. Once again, if they see anything of military interest they radio MFO HQ.

The Observers are separate from the military peacekeepers and consist of a team of civilians hired by the U.S. State Department. They patrol Zones A, B, and D via helicopter or, when necessary, by ground vehicle. They make notes on what they see in those areas in the way of military units and installations and once again send up a report to MFO HQ.

It's not terribly complicated as organizations go and it has worked very well, so far. So long as the sole concern is the two Treaty signatories and not a third-party trouble-maker.

I was SOPV for only a short time before the Next Big Thing came along. In this case, it was the change of command for the MFO. The current Force Commander, Major-General Martinelli, would be stepping down and returning

MODERN TRANSLATION

to Italy. There was to be a big ceremony at North Camp, which for me meant a lot of visitors to accommodate as well as the need to provide photography support.

Martinelli's replacement was going to be a Norwegian general. The different contingents take turns providing the commanding officer of the Force in some sort of complicated negotiations which go on who-knows-where.

There was a Fijian departure ceremony for Maj. Gen. Martinelli and his wife. I was one of the invited guests and found it very impressive. We sat on floor cushions in the Fijian's all-purpose hall. There were a lot of speeches and traditional gifts.

There was also a Kava ceremony which saw everyone taking turns drinking from a big bowl of the national drink of Fiji. I misunderstood and turned down the opportunity to partake as I thought the drink contained alcohol. I was lucky because the mixture is non-alcoholic but DOES have an effect similar to novocaine.

Afterwards the Martinellis were invited to stand in the back of one of the MFO pickup trucks. I noticed that there were thick ropes attached to the front bumpers and some of the big Fijians were picking them up.

A Fijian NCO looked at me and gestured at the rope. "Please, Sir!" That's when I realized we were to pull the truck to the Martinelli's around part of the camp, no small feat but apparently an MFO tradition. I could hardly turn down the Fijians since I had told them I couldn't drink Kava. I did my best pulling that rope but I honestly think the Fijians were doing most of the work. Still, a good time was had by all.

The Colombians also did a ceremony. This was held outdoors and included a traditional dance known as the "Colomba." Couples performed the dance while wielding torches. The Colombians also did a presentation in full combat gear, simulating a patrol while someone read a patriotic speech written by a Colombian soldier on the eve of his death. The ceremony was both impressive and scary at the same time.

Meantime, I was dealing with some personnel turbulence of my own. The Canadian and Colombian contingent commanders were taking away my driver and translator, respectively. These positions were not going to be filled. Because of all the work we were already saddled with I had to wait until after the change of command before I could discuss these changes with the command group.

When I finally saw the November-December issue of the Sandpaper I found out it was as bad as I thought it would be. The magazine was full of "dead space," including blank pages. The photography was mediocre. Cutlines were

FRENCH INTERLUDE

poorly written or missing. The magazine had an overall feel of something that was simply thrown together.

"What do you want to do with them, Sir?" asked my Fijian NCO.

I shrugged. I knew that the racks for the magazines had been empty for months. The magazines, such as they were, had been paid for and the money could not be recouped. "Go ahead and distribute them."

I knew that almost ANYTHING we put out at this point would be an improvement. In fact, I was planning to take advantage of the disruption of our printing schedule to do a special 25th issue of the Sandpaper. At the very least the issue would make a great souvenir for the peacekeepers

We had the first of a several deaths during my term in the Sinai. Several Egyptian contract workers were traveling home on the Mediterranean Road in an auto when they crashed; no one survived that accident.

In the States a military-related accident would result in some kind of media coverage. Not in the Sinai. Vehicle fatalities were too common in Egypt, apparently, and only Xinhua, the Chinese news service, picked up the event and played up the MFO angle.

I was surprised and disturbed to discover how many people were crammed into the vehicle and how far they were traveling in order to work in the dining facility at North Camp. The desperate need for jobs stems, ironically, a direct result of the Egyptian government's attempt to "guarantee" jobs. Today, ANY job will do and with two or three you might just get by, considering how little money an Egyptian job provides.

I had a meeting with the new Force Commander, Maj. Gen. Kjell Narve Ludvigsen. When I went in his office he had a protractor and ruler and was doing something to a map.

He looked up at me. "Do you know we are within rocket range of Gaza?"

I was taken a little aback. Yes, I had noticed that the latest rockets being fired at Israel from the Gaza strip seemed to have the capability to hit North Camp... in theory. If the rockets were fired from the southern corner.

Anyway, it showed that the general was already monitoring an issue which concerned the Israelis, the Egyptians and the MFO: Hamas.

The MFO watches the Gaza-Egyptian border, as this was stipulated by the Treaty. There was once a beach near the border town of Rafah where peacekeepers could relax and swim in the Mediterranean. When Peacekeepers traveled to Tel Aviv from North Camp in the 1980s it was possible to drive the shortest route: straight through the Strip.

That was not the case in 2007 because in 1994 a deal was worked out called the Oslo Accords. This agreement would hand over Gaza and the West

Blackhawk helicopter coming in for a landing at North Camp. US Army
helicopters of the AVCO provide valuable service in the Sinai, shuttling
Force members to OPs, providing the Observers an aerial view of military
installations and providing a MEDEVAC capability when needed.

Bank from Israeli control and give to the Palestinian Authority. In exchange, the Palestinian Authority would actively prevent terror attacks on Israel.

Unfortunately, the PA's ruling Fatah Party turned out to be totally corrupt and incompetent. Fatah managed to alienate many of the Palestinians who lived in the two territories. Worse, the Palestinian Authority either would not or could not meet its part of the Oslo Accords when it came to terror attacks, which included suicide bombers and rockets launched by the Hamas "party."

Hamas, whose charter states that it will "continue until Israel is obliterated," won the 2006 elections in Gaza. Hamas had begun a civil war in Gaza only a few weeks before I arrived against Fatah. In the meantime, it was still finding the time to fire rockets at Israeli towns. And maybe us.

My meeting with General Ludvigsen was pretty productive. I explained what I did and what I didn't do. He was very interested in the Sandpaper. He asked me if I had a copy.

The LAST thing wanted to do was show him the November issue. I might have said something about problems with the printers or something but I know I didn't promise to show him that issue! I would have rather gone to the Gaza border and wave an Israeli flag from the wall.

# THE CHEERLEADER GIG

## 3

Before I even had a chance to really get a handle on my new job I was hit by several things in short order.

First and foremost was the Bengal Cheerleaders visit arranged by Armed Forces Entertainment. They were scheduled to do a tour of the troops in the Sinai as part of the AFE Mediterranean circuit. Now I never had to deal with AFE visits before in any job I did for the Army so this was a serious learning curve for me, getting clearances done, arranging for venues for their shows, meals, billeting etc. etc. On top of all this I am NOT a sports person. I was only vaguely aware that the Bengals were an American football team.

Instead of trying to hide the fact that I was going to be escorting the cheerleaders around the Sinai I decided to come right out and tell Heidi about. I thought she would see the irony of the situation and get a laugh out of it.

"You're going to WHAT?!" I heard her say, very loudly over the phone. She was not laughing.

Lieutenant Sutherland, my Canadian sidekick, volunteered to take the escort mission. This relieved me to no end. Now I could concentrate on learning the ins and outs of the Visits part of the job. Besides I wanted to find if my unaccompanied baggage had arrived in Tel Aviv. While I was at it I emailed Heidi to tell her the good news: that her husband wouldn't be hanging around a bunch of cheerleaders.

My relief was short-lived when I found myself in a meeting just two days before we were scheduled to pick up the Ben-Gals in the Canal Zone. I found out that Sutherland could not escort the cheerleaders after all because he had to play in an important field hockey game (!) for the Canadian team. Apparently Canadians take hockey very seriously and will play even in the desert.

But then again, the U.S. Contingent seemed to be *obsessed* with this cheerleader visit. All I suggested was that there must be someone better for the job: someone who knows sports, someone who knows the Sinai better, and most of all someone who isn't *married.* But when I stressed the dilemma of not having Sutherland available to do the pickup instead of sympathy what I got was Colonel Parks, U.S. Army, saying "then YOU do it."

The entire room was quiet. "I don't see a problem with that, do you?" Parks asked. Actually, I could see several problems with it, one of which

## INCREASING
## MORALE

being I would have to call Heidi AGAIN and tell her that I would indeed be traveling with the cheerleaders after all. But he clearly wasn't interested in MY problems. "No, Sir." I replied.

Even though I was an MFO staff officer working directly for the Force Commander I did, of course, belong to Task Force Sinai, composed of the 1SB and the USBATT. The United States Battalion observes and reports activities in the southern sector of Zone Charlie from their remote site positions. These battalions rotate and when I arrived it was the 2nd of the 230th Field Artillery Regiment (Kansas Army National Guard).

The U.S. Army's 1st Support Battalion, or 1SB, is an integral part of the MFO, providing the needed logistics (or at least making sure the logistics happen) to keep the Force operating in the desert. Aviation, medical assets, mail and finance services for all United States personnel go through this unit and other support is provided for the Contingents of the Multinational Force and Observers.

In any case, now that the rose was pinned on me I had to get everything up and running for the visit. I had more paperwork to do. I had to make reservations in Cairo at one of the three MFO-approved hotels. And I had to tell Heidi about the change in plans, even though some of the other staff members I worked with pointed out that there was no way she would know if I didn't tell her. But I figured she would understand.

"You're STILL picking up the cheerleaders?!" She asked. She did NOT understand.

Because my Canadian driver had been withdrawn I had to arrange for a rented car and an Egyptian driver. We began our trip from the front gate at North Camp and it rapidly became clear to me that the driver knew virtually no English. I could only hope that he was actually taking me to my hotel in Cairo.

We had an interesting time traveling up to the Mediterranean coast, dodging potholes and stopping at various police checkpoints along the way. In the distance were a few Bedouins and their camels, the occasional farm claimed from the desert, a half-finished house with columns sticking up into the sky.

During my time as a peacekeeper I could never understand why there were so many half-finished buildings in Egypt. The answer is really quite simple: taxes. The government doesn't tax houses until they are complete. So if you want a two-story house in Egypt you fill out the paperwork for a three-story one... and just never finish the top floor.

Once we reached al-Arish and its mix of new and old buildings the road improved rapidly. It was comforting to see Coca-Cola logos on some of the stores, this close to Hamastan. We drove along the sea for a while.

35

# LOST
# BAGGAGE

Donkey carts are obviously still a big part of the transportation infrastructure in this part of the world, and you see the small animals pulling a variety of loads. I saw more camels, including one that a Bedo was trying to convince to climb into the back of his pickup truck.

Arab drivers are notorious and there were several times when I was sure that an oncoming truck or car was not going to swerve back to their lane in time. It was hard not to think of the workers who had died on this stretch of road not that long ago.

When I was in Saudi Arabia during Operation Southern Watch we used to say that the Iranians believed that if you died in a holy war you would go straight to Heaven... but the Saudis believed if you died behind the wheel of a pickup truck you would go to Paradise. It looked to me as if their Bedouin cousins belonged to the same Muslim denomination.

The number of bad drivers increased as we got closer to the Suez Canal. We crossed it on the Mubarak Peace Bridge, a spectacular structure built by the Japanese. The canal used to be the crossroads between Europe and Asia, between Britain and India, between the Middle East and Africa. There is still a lot of traffic along it but it doesn't have the strategic importance it used to.

The Suez Canal is truly a remarkable feat of engineering, especially when you consider that the original work took place in the 19th century. Using steam power a French visionary, or madman, dug the canal connecting the Mediterranean to the Red Sea and the Indian Ocean.

By cutting a canal here ships are saved an additional 4,300 miles of travel between India and Europe, since it cuts out a long trip around Africa. When first built the canal could easily handle the largest vessels then afloat.

Of course, the construction of the Canal immediately made it a strategic asset. The Canal allows rapid shipment of oil from the Middle East to Europe, its biggest customer. It also allows for the rapid transit of warships... if you control it or at least have access to it. During WWI the Central Powers made a serious effort to take it from the east but didn't have enough resources. During WWII Rommel wanted to capture it from the west but the Afrika Korps couldn't quite make it. The 1956 War was fought for control of the Suez Canal. The 1973 War was launched from one side of the canal to the other and then back again.

Today Egypt hosts two Wonders of the World: the Pyramids, one of the Seven Ancient Wonders (and the only one which still exists from that group) and the Suez Canal, one of the Modern Wonders of the World.

We stopped near the town of Ismailia. The driver had his car washed and I had the opportunity to get a Coke and a pastry that can only be described as a "super ding-dong." The driver got some gas, I took a few pictures, and we were off again.

# SOLDIERS AND LOCALS

The Canadian flag detail at one of the MFO's many ceremonies. Canada has been vigorously involved in peacekeeping since the end of WWII , participating in over 30 operations. In the 35 years of the MFO Canada has done everything from operating in the Rotary Wing Aviation Unit to serving in the Force Military Police Unit. Canadians have also played key roles on the Force staff and in administration.

We next passed near a huge monument of a bayonet sticking straight up into the sky, a reminder of the vicious fighting here during the 1973 War. There were military installations nearby as well and they had monuments in front of their gates. The fight for the Canal is still very much on the minds of the locals.

The things named after Mubarak and Mubarak pictures increased exponentially as we got closer to Cairo. He definitely had a cult of personality going for him, with portraits (some of them billboard-sized) gracing several buildings, town entrances, and even random places along the highway. Mubarak got credit on the nightly news for anything that went right. His photos looked down on you whenever you were in a public building. He evidently had learned a thing or two from fellow dictator Saddam Hussein, except he never got around to putting his face on any banknotes.

We followed a small canal for a while, then crossed open desert, then the outskirts of Cairo, and finally the big city itself. Traffic was painfully bad, with drivers trying to squeeze five lanes of traffic into four, resulting in occasional failures. Police attempted to direct traffic at intersections, with varying levels of success. Cairo appears to have over 18 million people but only one traffic light.

I don't know what I was expecting. I guess I was disappointed that this was not the Cairo of Raiders of the Lost Ark. You were in more danger of being run down by a Toyota than finding yourself in a sword fight.

I arrived at the Mövenpick Hotel. I really wondered whether or not the Egyptians might be trying to solve their unemployment problems by putting every adult male in a police uniform. In addition to the regular police there were tourism police officers assigned to regulate access to the hotel and security guards to keep an eye on the grounds and inside the hotel.

The hotel was very nice, with a book store, gift shops and a couple of restaurants. There was even a store where you could get Omar Sharif-brand shirts, in case I want something to wear at a special showing of Dr. Zhivago, or maybe Lawrence of Arabia. Then again, do I really want to go around telling people I wear Omar Sharif's shirts? It makes it sound like I went to a Cairo yard sale.

There was a 3-piece ensemble playing in the lobby that was very good and relaxing to listen to. This is more than could be said for the discotheque which was apparently located on the floor above my room. This made getting a good night's sleep very difficult.

The next morning I began Phase II of Operation Cheerleader... I collected the Dahab bus in front of the hotel and proceeded to Suez. This drive was uneventful, once we were clear of the city. Lots of military installations along the way but (officially) nothing of any interest to me as a peacekeeper since they were on the western side of the Canal.

I met the Ben-Gals at a drop-off point in Suez. They were very polite and enthusiastic and dressed in warm-up suits, which was a load off my mind. Egypt isn't Saudi Arabia but hanging around Suez in the kind of things cheerleaders wear for games would have just been asking for trouble.

And we already had casualties: one of the cheerleaders hurt her ankle while doing a show the night before. Another was having gastrointestinal problems. Since I had no medic all we could do was make them comfortable until we reached South Camp and had them looked at by our medical personnel there.

They loaded up in my bus and we were on our way to South Camp, driving through the Suez tunnel to return to the Asian side of the Canal. This route took us along the Red Sea and we passed Ayun Musa. In this part of the world it is impossible to avoid being reminded that this is Holy land, and in the case of Ayun Musa, or the Spring of Moses, there is a story that during the Exodus the Israelites stopped here following the parting of the Red Sea. The Israelites and their flocks desperately needed water but the spring was undrinkable until Moses made a miracle. Now tourists can stop and get a drink but from what I've heard Moses's miracle only made it drinkable... not tasty.

I'll stick to Bebsi.

Most of the route was barren, with just the occasional petrol station and snack bar. At the Egyptian police checkpoints we occasionally passed I learned my first Arabic word. Every place we stopped a police officer would step into the bus, look around, and say *"Ashra..."* or ten. Ten? There were more than ten of us on the bus. Which ten? OVER ten? Apparently in this laid back part of Egypt the details are not that important.

During the trip some of the Ben-Gals took the opportunity to crash out while others chattered amongst themselves. The day before they got a tour of the Pyramids and some of them had even ridden camels. They were certainly getting the full tourist treatment while they were in Egypt.

We drove near the entrance to Ras Muhammad National Park as we cut across the tip of the peninsula to Sharm el-Sheikh, or just Sharm to most peacekeepers. Once a small fishing village, Sharm is now a resort city and a former presidential retreat for Mubarak. The Italian patrol boat facility and South Camp were once lonely seaside outposts but now are virtually surrounded by casinos, hotels and beaches. The waters teem with pleasure craft and the streets host gift shops, at least one bowling alley, a Hard Rock Café and a Planet Hollywood.

# DEEP IN THE
# DESERT

Two U.S. Army soldiers in Dress Greens in front of the Memorial Arch
(ACUs or DCUs were every day dress). The Memorial Arch commemorates
those peacekeepers and associated personnel who have died while serving
in the Sinai.

South Camp is much smaller than North Camp and does not have as many amenities but it makes up for it with the VIEW. Looking out over the sea you can see Tiran Island in the distance and of course the water activities in the Gulf of Aqaba, including parasailing. There are also signs warning of sharks but hey, you can't have everything.

This was my first visit to South Camp and it was doomed to be a short, busy one. I met up with Major Candelario (my "go-to" guy for South Camp) and we got the Ben-Gal's gear over to the barracks we put aside for their sole use and showed them the outdoor stage where they would be doing tonight's show. They seemed pretty happy and started practicing their routine.

The show was a great success. Only a couple of hundred soldiers of the USBATT and a few representatives of the other contingents were there for the show but what they lacked in numbers they made up for in enthusiasm as the Ben-Gals danced, changed costumes, did funny routines and encouraged audience participation.

We had trouble getting the cheerleaders away from the stage since so many soldiers wanted to get their pictures taken with them. We moved on to the Sportsman's Bar, a kind of soldier's canteen, but had the same problem when it came to getting them out of there. Finally, we managed to get them back to their barracks around midnight and I could take a break from being chaperone... at least I did until we found out that the Ben-Gals had no towels. The kind of visitors the MFO normally gets (i.e., military personnel in transit) normally bring their own.

The Ben-Gals apparently were in the showers even as we spoke with their representative at the door... but had no way of drying themselves. Or covering themselves. "We don't have a THING to wear," she said, with just her head sticking out.

In the interest of public safety we needed to get this problem resolved as quickly and as quietly as possible. We had to open up the Force Exchange and "borrowed" towels from the shelves with the understanding that they would be thoroughly laundered, folded, and placed back in stock with no one the wiser.

The next morning we had a few odds and ends to take care of. We had breakfast and more pictures, this time with the crew of the U.S. Army helicopter stationed at the South Camp helipad. Then we drove out to the airport where a French aircrew was waiting to fly us to North Camp.

The aircraft we were taking was a Twin Otter bush plane. I hadn't seen a bush plane since I lived in Alaska but as aircraft went this one had a good reputation. The six French crewman and cheerleaders pretty much filled the

# SHOW
# BIZ

plane (good thing we sent the baggage ahead on the bus) and we puttered around the big jetliners on the tarmac until we found the runway and took off.

Our course brought us right up the Gulf of Aqaba: Egypt on our left, Saudi Arabia on our right and water right underneath us. I saw tankers sailing to and from the ports on the far end of the Gulf. The reefs were clearly visible beneath the waves and there were more Egyptian resorts. There was also Pharaoh's Island and the remains of a European-style castle, a reminder of the days of the Crusader Kingdoms in the Holy Land.

As we flew along we would occasionally bank left or right slightly. Now at one point I started the process to get a civilian pilot's license so I know a little bit about flying and I couldn't figure out what all these adjustments to our course were about... until I saw one of the cheerleaders coming out of the cockpit. It seemed that the French pilots, being pilots, were showing off for the cheerleaders by giving them impromptu flying lessons.

We banked hard left and headed north, crossing over some low mountains. We were flying low enough to see wadis blocked with stone, the trapped rainwater allowing grass to grow for the occasional sheep. We saw Bedo shelters (but no Bedouins) and even areas covered with tracks from tank treads... maybe a reminder of one of the wars fought here over the last 50 years since no tanks have been in this part of Sinai since 1982.

We arrived around 1200. I had literally just completed a tour around all three sides of the Sinai "triangle." And this mission STILL wasn't over.

The tour of North Camp went over even better than at South Camp. More photos and an impromptu show at the Dry Cactus, the main recreation center. Unfortunately the Colombians mobbed the cheerleaders during a lull and wanted photos and autographs. I was worried for a moment that the Hungarian MPs would have to step in and restore order. Part of the problem was that each cheerleader had their own "collector card" featuring a photo and some stats and they were passing these things out to everyone who wanted one. The Colombians were damn keen on getting the entire set.

Finally handed off the Ben-Gals to Lt. Sutherland and they hit the road that evening at 2100, heading for their next engagement by way of Cairo. All I can say is that I can live without all the excitement that comes with show business. Give me gunfire and the occasional rocket any day.

# THE BIG DIG

# 4

Despite just being there I found myself on a flight to go back to South Camp, this after barely having time to check on my unaccompanied baggage. I had some photography gear I wanted to use in the Sinai but for some reason my stuff isn't in Tel Aviv yet.

1st Theater Sustainment Command, the higher headquarters for 1SB, was sending an inspection team to look at the USBATT setup and they want the staff officers from Task Force Sinai to be there "in case they have any questions." Since 1st TSC didn't send their Public Affairs Officer it seemed highly unlikely that their Engineer Officer is going to ask "Hey... what about those Talking Points, huh?"

Normally when these kind of things happen I just go with the flow but while I was pointing out the scarce flora and fauna of the southern Sinai to the Cheerleaders nothing got done. No progress had been made on the Sandpaper magazine, even though it was supposed to be ready in a few days, and Sutherland couldn't do much on the Visits side because he was busy with CANCON business. I got in touch with him in Cairo by phone, confirmed that the battle handoff on the Ben-Gals had been made, and asked him to get back to North Camp to get everything running again in Visits and told my journalist-NCO to finish the layout by the time I got back or we would BOTH be staying in the SOPV building until it was finished.

So there I was, sitting at the airfield, waiting for the rest of the staff to show up. I got my ukulele out and played a few chords on it. Colonel Woods, the Task Force commander, arrived and began talking about how someone was giving him a sob story. He went on and on until I stopped playing my uke and offered it to him. "It's not the world's smallest violin, but it'll do." I told him.

He just looked at me dumbstruck. Then he slowly turned away from me. I could tell he wanted to laugh.

We piled into the Twin Otter and as soon as the door was closed the plane started taxiing down the runway. The female sergeant sitting next to me said "Well, I guess there isn't going to be a safety briefing about what to do in case of a crash or if the oxygen masks drop."

# AIR
## ACTIVITY

I looked up at the oxygen-mask free ceiling of the aircraft. Then I looked at her. "I think you might have a misconception as to just how high this kind of plane flies."

And sure enough, as we were flying south I watched the shadow of the Twin Otter passing on the barren ground below. Then I noticed dots passing across the shadow of the airplane and my mind could not wrap itself around the problem of these shadows and being unable to see the source between the Twin Otter and the ground... until I got the idea to look up and saw the source was a flock of birds ABOVE us. We were flying lower than the birds.

There are two aviation units in the MFO: the RWAU, or Rotary-Wing Aviation Unit, and the Fixed Wing Aviation Unit (FWAU). The RWAU has been provided by several contingents, including Australia and Canada. Currently, the mission is conducted by a U.S. Army Aviation unit (AVCO) and provides a medevac capability, the means to do observation throughout the Sinai and the ability to reach any of the OPs relatively quickly for resupply or emergencies. The FWAU has since been incorporated into the AVCO.

The FWAU is a French unit and it provides transportation between North Camp and South Camp. Larger aircraft used to be employed for getting supplies and personnel between the two bases but by my tour the French Air Force operated a single DHC-6 Twin Otter, capable of flying over a dozen passengers and their gear... provided their gear isn't that heavy.

Of course, there is only a helipad at South Camp so the Twin Otter lands at the Sharm el-Sheikh International Airport when delivering people to South Camp and ground transport takes over from there. All in all, it's the quick way to get from north to south and vise-versa. There's also the bus, as I would find out when a sandstorm hit.

This particular flight was uneventful until we arrived in the area around Sharm. We flew in a very wide arc over the Gulf of Aqaba (I could swear at one point we must have been in Saudi airspace) in order to follow the vector given to us by the air traffic controller. It seemed that Mubarak was in town and extra security measures were in place, although this being Zone C I'm not sure what that would mean if active countermeasures were needed. I believe antiaircraft guns are *verboten* under the terms of the Treaty.

Once we were on the ground the plane was put in its shed (I would hardly call the structure a "hanger") and we piled in SUVs to drive down the Peace Road to South Camp. The Peace Road was lined with black-uniformed police every 100 yards or so, which seemed to confirm the impression we had that the President of Egypt was staying in Sharm. All I know is that many cops did a lot towards reinforcing the peaceful nature of the road.

We stopped at one point and the French airmen climbed out and went to get a taxi. They had an apartment in Sharm that they used when they overnighted. They would not be spending a night in temporary billets on the base, eating the hot dogs and the Coca-Cola, *absolument pas*!

This visit to South Camp was much less hectic and far less aggravating. I checked into the Sinai Inn billets, changed into civvies, and went to an inbrief regarding the inspection. Then I went over to the Hungarian Bar with Massimo (an Italian officer on the MFO staff) and others to unwind.

Over the next few days I really got to know South Camp. Although North Camp is bigger it also feels more isolated. In South Camp you can food delivered to the front gate… even McDonald's. South Camp has a seaside view but the facilities, such as the library and the exchange, are much smaller than North Camp's. But South Camp has one ace that North Camp can't touch and that's the fact that it has its own beach.

I met Herb for the first time while I was at the beach. The man was a living legend. An ex-Sergeant-Major in the U.S. Army, he was in charge of the recreation programs in South Camp and had been ever since the MFO was formed. He put out flyers with things printed on them like "Herb Says 'Everything Is Already Perfect. Sometimes We Are Just Too Blind To See It'" and "Herb Says 'Safety is Everybody's Responsibility.'" He had signs printed with his name on them and his swimming records ("Herb's Stats"). He had the steps leading to the beach ("Herb's beach") painted with his nuggets of wisdom. The South Camp physical fitness center had a sign over the door mentioning him ("Herb's Gym"). He lifted weights. He would hang upside down from an iron bar. He would swim all the way to Tiran Island when the mood hit him.

Herb's cult of personality might have been more localized than Mubarak's but that didn't make it any the less real.

And I suddenly found myself speaking to Herb, since someone told him I am the new SOPV. Herb was looking for new ways to spread the doctrine of Herbism and must have thought I could help him with articles in the Sandpaper, radio spots, etc.: "Sir, I have a lot of ideas, especially when it comes to integrating the mind and body… a sharp mind can't work without a sharp body…" and I think my brain blocked out the rest. It might have been a reflex, a fallback to my Cold War training I received on how to avoid brainwashing if captured, but I knew I couldn't resist forever.

"Hey, this sounds like a health issue." I pointed to another officer, my new roommate in fact. "You see that guy over there? That's the new Surgeon. I'll bet he would LOVE to hear about your ideas."

So Herb went over to bend the ear of our medical officer. Later on he arrived in the dining facility and said in a loud voice "OK, which one of you

FINE DINING

rascals fingered me to Herb?!" Oh wait, he may not have used the word "rascals." He might have used something a bit stronger.

The inspection closed out, no real surprises and certainly no concerns for the Public Affairs side. Another trip to the Hungarian Bar and Massimo demonstrated his skills at ping-pong. He beat all comers. He offered to play while holding one foot in his hand but by then no one was in the mood to get trounced again.

Later, at the dining facility, a bunch of us staff officers sat together and talked shop. Someone mentioned Herb.

"If I was down here I'd be making up fake Herb flyers," I said. "'Herb Says the Fastest Way between Two Points Is a Straight Line' or 'Herb Says A Penny Saved is a Penny Earned.'"

I got a few laughs among my peers for suggesting it but of course, I didn't do it for a really good reason: "Herb Says He Can Still Kick Anyone's Butt at South Camp."

I had a chance to go down to the beach, first to do Water Survival Training and then to just relax. Water Survival training is a result of one of those odd Catch-22s that the Army is always creating. When soldiers were sent to the Persian Gulf area or Iraq or Afghanistan they got additional pay known as Combat Zone Tax Exclusion, or CZTE. However, soldiers in the Sinai desert are NOT authorized CZTE because in the hallowed halls of the Pentagon it was determined that the Sinai is not a "combat zone," despite the admittedly rare terrorist attack in Sharm el Sheikh or even near North Camp itself. The same people also determined that the Red Sea IS a Combat Zone.

So, every few months U.S. soldiers would fly down to Sharm and proceed to Herb's Beach for WST. The amount of money CZTE involved was no small amount (especially for officers) so we would swim out about 10-20 feet from the shore (and actually AWAY from the danger, unless al-Qaida is training suicide tuna) and do all manner of training meant to keep you alive in the water.

I was doing WST Level 0, which consisted of holding station in the water in full uniform while holding a rifle and floating on my back. Yes, it does sound like some kind of a bizarre dare. I did OK until the "confidence building" portion of the training, in which we were required to curl up into a ball and float for a bit with my head underwater. I was wearing swim goggles which quickly filled up with seawater, which blinded me. Trying to float AND hold on to my rifle AND clear the goggles proved to be too much for me but it must have been entertaining to watch from the shore. Waves and jellyfish made the job even more difficult.

A quick shower and time spent rinsing the saltwater out of my ACUs and I was back in the beach in my shorts and with my gig bag. The jellyfish were no

SIGHT-SEEING
ON THE BEACH

longer around and I sat on the sand and began practicing "Tom Dooley" on my ukulele. The General and his wife were nearby, enjoying the sun and sand, and got up and left shortly after I started playing. I tried not to take that personally.

I next tried snorkeling, having borrowed the kit from the nearby equipment hut. I was amazed at the variety of fish just a few feet from the shoreline. My father once kept a saltwater aquarium and I recognized many of the species as being very sought-after by tropical fish aficionados. The coral reef comes almost right up to the beach so it's no surprise that so many colorful fish would be nearby.

I had to take the bus back to North Camp. This was yet another adventure. The route was roughly along Gulf of Aqaba to the Israeli border and then followed the border to El Gorah... except that the road doesn't exactly hug the shoreline, rather it weaves through the hills in the south which slows things down a bit. And the route along the Egyptian-Israeli border has several roadblocks manned by Egyptian border guards.

The hills had a few Bedouin settlements here and there but the area was so desolate that I wondered how anyone could live there. Not a tree, not a bush, not a blade of grass. This area made North Sinai look like Yosemite National Forest by comparison. The coast wasn't much better, with what appeared to be abandoned seaside resorts, or at least they were having a bad tourist season.

We stopped at the Shark Bay overlook, which served as the midpoint rest stop. As a rest stop it didn't have much in the way of conveniences. I took a few pictures, paid a pound to use the restroom (which seemed to be the going rate) and bought come cookies to go with the box lunch we each were provided. This was pretty much the entire Shark Bay Experience.

Along the Israeli-Egyptian border we saw guard posts for both sides. The Egyptian posts were tiny bases made of concrete... the platoon stationed at the post would put up road blocks consisting of oil drums and other junk. They would stop us and board the bus for a few minutes and then pass us on. The landscape was empty; the border guards probably just stopped vehicles to have something to do.

We stopped again, this time at one of the Colombian OPs for a rest break. OPs consist of an observation tower, a radio antenna and a couple of prefab buildings for the peacekeepers. Their billets, dining facility, exercise equipment, radio room and other gear was contained within a fenced-in perimeter. No two sites are exactly the same.

In addition to the human peacekeepers there were also dogs kept at the OPs. Each was authorized up to three animals and they provide companionship for the soldiers while they are stuck in the empty desert. They also filled another

French aircrew conduct a preflight check on the DHC-6 Twin Otter prior to departing North Camp for Sharm el-Sheikh. Twin Otters have a proven record around the world as bush aircraft and light transports and the French aircrews were very professional.

Colombians following a medal parade. In addition to an infantry battalion, the Colombians provide vital medical and dental personnel.

function: they are very good watchdogs. In a land where a the Bedo will take anything that sits unattended too long it is very helpful to have a dog who can sense them well before they get to the fence.

The MFO gets the dogs from the Egyptian Society for the Prevention of Cruelty to Animals. Most Arabs detest dogs and consider them unclean. It is the equivalent of one winning the lottery to become an MFO Remote Site mascot, with three meals a day, a comfy place to sleep, vet care for the rest of its life and people to love them.

We passed more Egyptian outposts on the way north. I was told that the Egyptian Army soldiers chosen for border guard duty were indeed unfortunates. Their families had no money or pull to get them assigned elsewhere in Egypt. Outposts were only occasionally visited by their leadership.

To the east, past the fence, was the Israeli side of the border. Guard towers here and there watched the area, serviced by a parallel road that was occasionally visible. On one spot there was an Israeli tower on one side of the fence and an Egyptian tower on the other, just a few meters from each other. You knew which was which because each had a national flag painted on its side. It looked like something out of the Cold War.

Back at North Camp I finally got back to work on my favorite part of the job… the magazine! Despite several meetings (I attended Force-level staff meetings and Task Force Sinai meetings) I was able to spend time on the Sandpaper which, despite what I was told over the phone, was NOT done. I wasn't too concerned at first.

Then the computer screwed up.

The computer we operated was one none of us was familiar with. We had the entire magazine laid out, but then the computer converted the entire thing to a Quark Xpress file… which the computer doesn't read!

Modern technology leaves me in awe. Computers today can create files for applications they don't have installed. And it wasn't like I had tech support at my fingertips… nobody in Rafah or al-Arish was likely to have a better grasp of the program than we did… and in Gaza they might know how to make a mean bomb but publishing software was a little out of their league.

A Force computer technician did manage to install a demo version of Quark Xpress… which allowed us to SEE the almost-completed product but not actually edit it. At least we were able to use our completed work as a template for reconstructing the entire thing in a new file. This added time in getting it to the publisher but we were able to make improvements on it and almost anything would have been better than what HAD been getting published. A lot of late nights were spent working on the magazine over the Easter weekend. We had more problems with the software.

58

## B.C. BLITZKRIEG

I had to leave the magazine to my NCO while I met the Military Attachés Group which was touring the Sinai. These officers, assigned to various embassies, flew in an Egyptian Air Force C-130 with their families. Wearing civilian clothes, the attachés were driven to see the Rafah crossing at the Egyptian-Gaza border wall. I arranged for family members to look around North Camp a bit and to go to the recreation hall but there really wasn't much to see during the work day. The visit ended up being a little longer than we expected when the military officers came back via the longer route.

I suppose this is all part of the job of being the military attaché: seeing for yourself what is going on so you can provide a first-hand report to someone or other.

I prepared to go one leave, a trip to Hawaii which had been planned months before I knew I was going to the Sinai. The magazine wasn't quite ready, and work only seemed to really get done when I was in close proximity to the layout process, but I had confidence that finished magazine was so close to completion that it would be finished by the time I got back.

# THE TWIN OTTER DISASTER $5$

Getting back from Hawaii was an adventure by itself. Honolulu to San Francisco to Amsterdam to Cairo. The gate number for the plane wasn't on my ticket or on any of the monitors in San Francisco. Impossible to get to sleep in Amsterdam. An hour to get through customs and immigration in Cairo, even though all my papers were in order.

And another surprise: no reservations at any of the MFO-approved hotels. I wound up staying at the Baron Hotel in Heliopolis, an area known for the architecture of the buildings constructed a hundred years ago. The Baron looked a little run down but it was comfortable and at that point all I wanted was a bath and a bed.

The next morning I got up and took some photos of the area. Across the street is the Baron Empain's Palace, a fantastic building which looked like a mix between Late Victorian and the Temple of Doom (I half-expected to see a guy wearing a fedora and a bullwhip run out). I shot some of the local mosques as well but didn't wander far as I still had to get back to the Sinai.

After a cab ride which would have given Evil Knievel the heebie-jeebies I waited at the Sonesta Hotel for the regular bus run back to North Camp. It was running late and when it did show up the driver seemed to be pretty... indifferent. A handful of us got on board and then we picked up people at the Mövenpick and El Salaam, passing a UN marked vehicle along the way.

The temperature in the bus began to rise and it wasn't hard to figure out why... an access plate over the engine was open, right in the aisle. The driver tried to ignore us while carbon monoxide began to fill the machine. He finally pulled over and fixed the thing.

Bus drivers came and went. The MFO contracted out the bus support and it seemed no one would do the job twice, even though so many people were looking for work. I suspect it had something to do with *baksheesh*, an Arabic term which could mean a tip, a handout, a kickback or a bribe... it's kind of a gray area in this part of the world. In all likelihood the MFO paid a set price for the service, including the driver's wages. The contractor in turn probably paid half of what was allocated and pocketed the rest. Even so, someone might have taken the job as a regular driver unless they were also paying for gas and other expenses out of pocket.

**ALI BABA
DESERT DELIVERY COMPANY
(Limited)**

I arrived back at North Camp to the same old issues. I was told that the crate with my missing gear in it might have been sighted in Cologne, Germany. By now the contents of my missing crate were reaching mystical proportions in my fevered imagination: I would be able to run faster, be smarter, do my job better if only I had my stuff.

May 6th, 2007 started out as a pretty uneventful day. I had breakfast, saw the French aircrew getting ready to go out, and later made my way to the Operations and Logistics meeting. There was nothing of any major concern going on at Force HQ, so I headed to my office.

I was working on my computer when I got a call to report to Colonel Parks. Immediately.

I walked the short distance back over to Headquarters. Other staff members were being called in. We were briefed on arrival that the Twin Otter was missing on its orientation flight to Saint Catherine's Monastery.

Now is a good time to talk about another quirk about life in the Sinai: no radar. The Treaty prohibits the MFO from using "sensors." This prohibition no doubt comes as a result of the Egyptian sensitivity to what it sees as "spying." Unfortunately, without radar the Flight Following Unit had to use math and guesswork to figure out where MFO aircraft were at any given time.

While I wrote up a press release stating that the Twin Otter was overdue and that we were doing everything we could to locate it and the crew. A UH60 was sent up to check the Twin Otter's route. Since the mission was an orientation flight the OPs were contacted to find out if they had seen the plane today. An Egyptian police report stated that an aircraft was seen near Nakhl attempting to make an emergency landing on the road.

Then the worst possible news came in: the UH60 spotted wreckage in a wadi. Major Morgan, a U.S. Army officer, was dropped at the crash site and was able to confirm that the wreckage was indeed the Twin Otter. There were no survivors.

We lost nine Peacekeepers that day: eight French and one Canadian.

I sat at my workstation in what passed for the Emergency Operations Center and began working on a new press statement. This was the one part of my job that I thoroughly disliked, but one that has to be done well. This situation, in particular, was sensitive since we had French, Canadian and Egyptian parties who had a stake in what was said over the next several hours. France and Canada would both need time to inform the families of the fallen peacekeepers.

And it wasn't long before I got the first phone call, this one from a Canadian media rep in Jerusalem who "heard that there had been an airplane crash."

"I have nothing more to add to the previous statement." I told her.

"Can you confirm that there was a Canadian national on board?"

Of course I couldn't. Families of every Canadian peacekeeper would be on edge if they knew that someone from their contingent MIGHT have been killed. "Please refer to the previous statement."

The reporter became exasperated. "Are you searching for the aircraft?"

"Please refer to the previous statement." I repeated, wondering where she was getting her information. Probably not direct, but through a Canadian member of the MFO calling or texting or emailing or blogging someone back home. When news stories came out they naturally got facts wrong, such as the one outlet which stated that the Twin Otter was "overloaded," but the MFO could not be singled out as the source of the bad info, not if I had anything to do with it.

We were able to put together a picture of at least some of the events which led to the loss of the Twin Otter before the French arrived with their investigative team. According to Egyptian eyewitnesses the aircraft was trailing smoke from one engine and may have been on fire when it attempted to land on a road near the village of el-Thamad, the only practical place to come down in the rough terrain. Unfortunately there was a truck driving on the road and one of the wings touched the roof before climbing back into the air. The pilot may have intended to come around and try again but she never made it: shortly afterwards the Twin Otter crashed.

The tragedy had a sobering effect on the Force, but the MFO is no stranger to death.

Near the Force Headquarters, in the area that serves as a parade ground for medal parades and other occasions, is a monument. It is small and understated but also oddly appropriate for a Force which is all about preventing war. It is the Memorial Arch, with its MFO emblem at the peak and the names of all the peacekeepers and associated personnel who died while in the service of the Multinational Force.

One of the first, and the largest, tragedies to befall the Force was the loss of Arrow Air Flight 1285 on December 12th, 1985. 236 soldiers of the elite 101st Air Assault Division ("Screaming Eagles") were returning home from a tour in the Sinai as the USBATT. Their chartered DC-8 stopped at Gander, Newfoundland to refuel for the last leg of their journey to Fort Campbell, Kentucky. All were killed when their jetliner crashed after takeoff. A total of 248 people lost their lives in the disaster, which some believe was due to the wings icing up.

I have heard other theories as well. One theory is that the place, which left from Cairo, was destroyed by a bomb put in place by terrorists (a claim was put in by a group called Islamic Jihad, a subsidiary of Hezbollah Corp.). There was also a rumor that someone in the 101st brought back a souvenir from the Sinai, which at that time had far more leftover mines and shells than it does now... someone might have thought that an old Russian shell or an Italian mine might make an interesting conversation piece.

It didn't help the rumor mill that the official Canadian investigation was "inconclusive."

The year before the Arrow Air disaster Mr. Leamon Hunt, the General Director of the MFO, was murdered in Rome, where the MFO Headquarters is located. His armored limousine was ambushed while waiting to enter the grounds of his residence; gunmen of the Red Brigades poured automatic fire into the vehicle until the fatal round managed to get through the glass.

The Red Brigades, although composed of cold-blooded communist killers, appeared to have no motive for killing the leader of the peacekeeping organization, although it is known that they had ties to the Palestinian Liberation Organization. The PLO certainly had no use for peace in the Sinai, peace in Gaza, or peace anywhere for that matter.

Other peacekeepers have lost their lives in the Sinai due to vehicle accidents. Driving in the Sinai is not for the fainthearted, due to road conditions and the temptation to drive at speeds higher than posted. On the al Arish-Qattara Road there are Arab drivers who might be considered obstacles rather than traffic and the occasional donkey cart and Bedo road block are nothing to be sneezed at either.

For our part, as peacekeepers on the road, we run into the problem of low-hanging wires. This is not dangerous to the MFO vehicle in the least but is a considerable public relations problem when homes and sometimes entire villages lose their telephone connection or electricity.

In the meantime we had to pick up the pieces and continue the mission. We would grieve for our fallen comrades but we would also get the job done. The Cairo Office planned an MFO 25th Anniversary Celebration for the day after the crash but none of the senior officers participated. Even if it was practical I think it would have felt wrong to drink champagne in Cairo while nine dead peacekeepers were in cold storage in North Camp.

Spot illustration for the memorial program for the Twin Otter crew.

Without the Twin Otter we had no air transport to South Camp unless we refueled the UH60s at one of the OPs, but this presented its own set of problems and as small as the Twin Otter was the UH60 wasn't a replacement in terms of capacity or speed. Plus it diverted the helicopters from their primary mission of supporting the Observers. The buses would have to pick up most of the freight between the camps.

The pace of my job became much faster as we had to clear whole new sets of visitors, none of whom we knew about only days or hours before and now they had to get clearance as quickly as possible to come to North Camp. Fortunately Rome, Cairo and Tel Aviv were doing their best to get investigators and other personnel into the Sinai. France sent a full-scale investigations team in a C-160 to look at the crash site, the aircraft debris and the human remains. They had forensics experts and mortuary affairs personnel. Canada also sent specialists.

I had to find billets for all these temporary personnel as well, and our spare capacity at North Camp was limited. We also provided VIP quarters to the French ambassador to Egypt when he came down for the memorial ceremony. In addition to the housing situation the French and Canadian experts needed our help with some of their documentation so they would be able to present identification to the Egyptian guards at the crash site.

We needed more mundane things too, like pre-crash photos of the fallen. No one other than SOPV at North Camp could produce quality photographs but these jobs were literally draining our ink cartridges dry and it wasn't as if I could go to the al-Arish Office Depot and buy replacements.

The French government was reviewing its commitment to the MFO. Would it send another Twin Otter? Only one French Air Force unit operated the type. Would it be wise to send as a replacement an aircraft identical to the one that crashed? Mechanical failure could not be ruled out and the same fate could befall a second Twin Otter as easily as the first.

Then we prepared to repatriate the nine bodies. We realized to our horror that our clinic did not have the means to store the remains of the peacekeepers killed in the accident. We had to improvise, utilizing a freezer van normally utilized for the storage of food for the dining facility. The van was emptied of all foodstuff and the remains were placed inside. Later it was thoroughly decontaminated.

I worked with Captain Young of the AUSCON on the memorial ceremony. We wound up putting much of our slim resources into it. Only four days after the disaster we had wreaths made of desert flowers placed on a table near the Memorial Arch, each one surrounding a photo of one of the fallen

The FRENCHCON commander saluting as one of the airmen of the Twin Otter is brought aboard a C-130 for the flight home. Each of the coffins was carried to the aircraft by members of a different contingent, in this case the COLBATT. Although the French and Canadians were the hardest hit, the deaths of these peacekeepers affected everyone to some degree or another.

peacekeepers. Flags from each contingent flew on the poles on one side of the parade ground... but the Canadian and French flags flew at half-mast.

The ceremony was conducted in French and English. The service records of each man and woman was read out loud. Prayers were said for the peacekeepers. It was all very solemn except for the occasional ring cell phone carried by one of our Egyptian guests... it seemed that they could not leave their phones off for more than 30 minutes.

The memorial ceremony ended with General Pons, the French Air Force Inspector, announcing that a new crew and another DHC-6 would be deployed to the Sinai. "Today the wind is from the desert, but tomorrow it will be from the new Twin Otter."

On May 12th we held a ramp ceremony to see off our fallen comrades. A detail from each contingent formed up on either side of the transport aircraft's rear ramp while a Fijian played "Taps" on a trumpet. Each set of remains was placed in a coffin and a pallbearers from the different contingents carried them into the hold one at a time. As each coffin passed the contingents they rendered a hand salute. Eight remains were draped with the French *tricolore* and the ninth with the Canadian Maple Leaf flag, or *l'Unifolié*.

I felt depressed afterwards. A lot of good people died in that crash and I guess it's hard to accept sometimes, even when you are a soldier.

The French investigation team did a very thorough job. Unfortunately the results were never shared with members of the Force. Was it mechanical? Was it the result of sabotage? Pilot error? A terrorist missile? So far as I can determine no public report was ever made.

I know better than most how easy it would be to bring down a relatively slow-moving aircraft like the Twin Otter, especially with a Stinger or an SA-7. But if Hamas was expanding its business into the Sinai it wasn't making a big deal out of it, which would have been uncharacteristic of them.

For better or worse, Arab cultures seems to thrive on rumors and conspiracy theories. I'm not sure why that is, unless it's just a method of explaining away the bad things that happen and assigning blame where you're more comfortable. Or in Egypt's case, it might be a form of paranoia leftover from when they were aligned with the Soviets.

For instance, Lebanon's civil strife has nothing to do with Hezbollah and their eternal "war" with Israel (and people who disagree with Hezbollah) but is a huge Mossad-CIA-British Secret Service plot to destroy one of the most beautiful places in the Middle East (James Bond himself was in on that one). Israel routinely trains birds to carry spy devices into Saudi territory. None of the 911 terrorists were Egyptian and the whole thing was done with "movie special effects."

Rumors floated around about the incident. One was that a mayday was picked up by an air traffic controller in the Canal Zone. With the radio aboard the aircraft this was impossible, but what do you expect from a region where it's not only possible to buy a copy of the Protocols of the Elders of Zion but people BELIEVE it.

Life rapidly returned to normal in North Camp. The new magazines came out, which everyone loved but which I felt could still be improved. Reports and meetings went on.

Every week there is a "Pizza Night" at the Rec Center. This is a fun deal where everyone contributes $3. You get half a ticket and the other half goes into a "cage." Then you make yourself a pizza from a small, pre-made raw crust and ingredients from a buffet-style bar. The kitchen staff bakes the pizza for you and the result is as good or as bad as you make it.

At the end of a night there is a drawing. The lucky person who has the winning ticket gets half the money raised; the other half covers the cost of the pizza stuff.

I got to the Rec Center early and there was no one there, just the cash box, the tickets and the wire cage for the drawing. I shrug my shoulders and put my three dollars in the box and got my tickets but before I could walk away from the table someone else came in. I wound up taking his money too and giving him a ticket until the next person came up....

I just intended to collect the money until whoever was in charge this week showed up. Each contingent takes turns and this week it was the Australians but after I collected over $150 it occurred to me that the Australians weren't going to show up and I was *de facto* responsible for tonight's drawing.

Oh well, SOMEONE had to be in charge I guess and I admit I had a little fun doing it. Not enough to volunteer to do it again but I guess it took my mind off what happened to the Twin Otter and its crew. So, after I had a chance to do my OWN pizza we did the drawing...

And Captain Young of the AUSCON won. Not an Aussie in sight until money was involved!

PIZZA NIGHT!

# 6

# A TRIP TO RAFAH

I had to face facts: I was never going to see my unaccompanied baggage again. My extra gear, my books, the tools of my public affairs craft were all gone. I had no choice but to submit a claim for my gear. As if mere money would replace my loss... if someone wanted to sabotage me they couldn't have done a better job of it.

In the meantime, things moved right along. Our next set of visitors was a delegation from the European Union. The EU folks wanted to come out and see first-hand the Gaza crossing at the Egyptian town of Rafah. Not only did I have to work out the normal documentation on each visitor but also arrange for transport and body armor for them to wear.

It started out all wrong. Arriving by road from the Nile Valley some of them went straight to OP 1A, along the Gaza border, which was according to plan. Others went to the front gate of North Camp because they were mistakenly directed there by Egyptian security. We got all that sorted out. Then we brought them to Rafah the next day.

Rafah is actually two towns now. It used to be mostly on the Gaza side of the border but now part of it is in Egyptian territory. The border crossing between Gaza and Egypt was established in 2005 with an understanding between Egypt, Israel and the Palestinian Authority that the crossing would be monitored by the EU so that only legitimate trade items and people could come in and out (in the meantime, Israel runs other crossings along their border for humanitarian aid). The European Union Border Assistance Mission at the Rafah Crossing Point (EU BAM Rafah) was created and almost won first prize for the World-Wide Multilingual and Multipurpose Euphemism and Acronym Contest (WWMMEAC) for 2006.

With Hamas in power this deal was in jeopardy. They didn't WANT impartial monitoring. Without unlimited and unmonitored border access how could they use Iranian weapons to kill Jews? Surely this was a violation of their inhuman rights.

Gaza is walled or fenced in all the way around... almost like the title city in Escape From New York, only without the skyscrapers and with slightly more deranged killers running about the streets. The wall on the Egyptian side is concrete, about 8 meters tall, and backed up by guard towers.

## SMUGGLING

Hamas is faced with two ways of subverting the control of illicit materials to Gaza. First is to use Public Relations Flotillas to try to break the Israeli-enforced Mediterranean blockade. This is a strategy in which Hamas, or its liberal elitist sympathizers in the United States and Europe, organizes ships to bring in humanitarian supplies. The PRF ships make a point of avoiding the Israelis, knowing that the Israelis will eventually have to board in order to make them change course. Once on board the "crew" offers physical resistance and the Israelis have to subdue them. This is caught on video by members of the PRF, heavily edited and of course given to sympathetic media agencies who spin it as "Mean Israelis Bash Defenseless Sailors Bringing in Baby Food."

Hamas hopes that the bad PR from these exercises will convince the Israelis that it's not worth it to stop the ships, which do indeed bring in humanitarian supplies... initially. But once the tap is opened the ships will bring in such humanitarian aid as rocket-propelled grenades, scud missiles and the occasional tank.

Unfortunately for Hamas the Israelis are standing firm so they've had to look to other means to undermine the blockade... literally. The construction of smuggling tunnels underneath the Egyptian border began. On any given day tunnels were being planned, dug and utilized to bring things in and out of Gaza.

The tunnels originate in the basements of some of the homes and other buildings in Gaza, then travel at depths of perhaps 100 feet. At that depth they are very difficult to detect. Some are quite sophisticated, using prefab cement sections and electrical lighting.

So while the European Union observers watched what was going at the official crossing point the Mole People were busy underground bringing ammunition, rockets, bomb components and bootleg copies of Borat into Gaza and bringing counterfeit $50 bills, propaganda videos, I *heart* Palestine *keffiyehs* and terrorists into Egypt.

You cannot look at the situation without pitying the Palestinians on the other side of that wall. They are in effect the largest collection of human shields on the planet. Saddam was an amateur, only collecting a handful of westerners to keep the Coalition from bombing him during Desert Shield... Hamas has collected well over a million. This way they can fire rockets and mortars randomly at the Israelis, occasionally killing someone minding their own business going to or from work or attending school. If the Israelis practice restraint then Hamas claims it as a victory. If the Israelis retaliate then the surviving Hamas members parade the bodies of civilians who didn't realize their apartment complex was sitting right next to the garage serving as the "Supreme High Command for the Liberation of the al-Aqsa Mosque (Limited)." The dead become martyrs to the cause and a reason for fashionable liberal elitists to hate

# NORWEGIAN 2007 NIGHT

## "WE HAVE OUR HATS...
## LET THE FESTIVITIES BEGIN!"

Israel. It also makes great fuel for the propaganda machines of Hamas, Hezbollah and Al-Jazeera.

I always felt that if the Greek government, out of the goodness of its heart, gave up one of its islands and evacuated it and offered it up as a new homeland for the Palestinians living in Gaza Hamas would machinegun Arabs on the beaches rather than let them leave the Gaza Strip. They would fire rockets at the ships waiting to take the Palestinians to their new homes. They would infiltrate suicide bombers on board the ships to prevent them from reaching their new home. Hamas defines its existence as "either we must die or the Israelis must die, there can be no compromise."

This is not exactly a good negotiating point. Without a civilian population to hide among Hamas would be quickly wiped out by the Israeli Defense Forces.

Each of the contingents celebrates one "national day" of its choice. In the case of Norway it is literally National Day, the day when Norway became an independent kingdom separate from Sweden and Denmark. Somehow, a whole shipment of plastic Viking helmets and sack cloths were arrived so that the North Camp community at large could celebrate.

There is something surreal about seeing dozens of Americans, Hungarians, Colombians, Fijians, Uruguayans, French, Kiwis and Australians all wearing horned helmets and brown sleeveless shirts, eating Norwegian food in the Sinai desert. Surreal but fun. General Ludvigsen presided over the event. He was wearing what looked like a real helmet and I might be mistaken but I thought he had a battle axe... he looked the part of a Viking chieftain.

When we were making arrangements for Viking Night there was a staff member from the Tel Aviv office who was trying to get himself invited to the festivities. I spoke to the next-highest ranking Norwegian officer to ask whether I should clear him to come in, since the guy was Danish and not Norwegian.

"Of course." He told me with a straight face. "What would Norwegian Day be without a Dane to beat up?"

This is apparently the punchline to a joke I never did get. Needless to say, no one really got beat up.

Even though there were only a handful of them the Norwegians were much a part of the team. They loved talking about their country and their culture. The lieutenant who was assigned to the MFO said that there was some odd "Russ Celebration" thing that takes place just before National Day. The celebration is something that students do when they graduate high school. I didn't quite understand the idea but it has something to do with dares, and his challenge came down to either walking into a pub completely naked or drinking an entire bottle of wine in five minutes or so.

Uruguayans on medals parade. This small country runs the TREU, responsible for civil engineering and ground transport functions in the MFO.

The Force Band. Tiny Fiji not only contributes the FIJIBATT but also provides the music needed for ceremonies.

"Which did you do?" one of us asked.

"Hey, it gets cold in Norway." He said. "I drank the wine."

"What else goes on during this Russ thing?" I asked.

"Well, there's a lot of singing of old, traditional Norwegian songs."

"Oh, you mean like 'let's sail to England, where we can rape-and-pillage-and-burn'..."

He just stared at me for a moment and then chuckled. We both know a little about Viking history.

I made progress with the Sandpaper. It was slow going but it was definitely getting there. This one was of particular importance since the cover story would be about the loss of the Twin Otter. I was so wrapped up in layout that I had to have Janan pick up the latest arrivals from Armed Forces Entertainment, a troupe of Polynesian dancers. The pickup had to be made at Ismailia on the west side of the Suez Canal.

The group arrived later than we planned, since for some reason Egyptian security forces were being more diligent than normal. We still had enough time to give them a little tour of the camp and to get everything set up for their show. They tried to show me how to play my personal ukulele but I seem to be the one person on Earth who can't play anything worth listening to on a uke.

The show was very well-received, especially among the Fijians. The troupe did dances from Hawaii, Tahiti and many of the smaller island groups. Afterwards the Fijians invited the dancers over for Cava.

The next morning it was a very rough group who boarded the bus for South Camp... but that's show business!

While we might be in the Middle East and in a buffer zone between two belligerents the Army pretty much treats it as just another assignment. So we had Army things we had to do.

One of them was to do a 12-mile ruck march. This is not as bad as it sounds, not once you're used to it. But in order to avoid the hottest part of the day Task Force Sinai roused us at 0355 in the morning. And it's not like you walk the 12 miles from Point A to Point B or to a hill in the distance and back... for security reasons it had to be around the inside perimeter of North Camp. So not only have you gotten up in the middle of the night but you're also walking around in circles (well, squares) over and over again. The only change in the scenery came from the differences in the lighting as the sun rose up over the desert.

URINALYSIS

This must have been no end of entertainment for the Colombians who manned the guard towers and watched us as we kept walking over the same ground over and over again, like a hamster in a wheel. A SQUARE wheel, no less.

A routine pickup became complicated when I went into Cairo to get Colonel Hedson at the airport. Hedson is the new Deputy Commanding Officer of the Task Force.

We waited in the lobby of the Mövenpick for a bit and discovered when it was time to leave that someone blocked our vehicle in the parking lot. Everyone was sympathetic to our plight but no one seemed to be able to find out who had the keys to the vehicle until I produced some money... *baksheesh*, of course. And it turned out that the Egyptian who I had been talking to for the previous five minutes was also the person who had blocked me and watched me try to get out of the lot.

The colonel's flight was delayed so we wound up driving all night to get to North Camp. It was extremely late so I kept the two pistols with me rather than spend an hour or two waking people up until I found someone who could open the arms room. The only thing that makes you feel safer than one pistol under your pillow while you're sleeping is two pistols under your pillow.

I was only a couple of months into my tour and I was already seeing off many of the Task Force people, even though by now I felt like I've been here at least as long as they have: Suqi, Andy, Anna, Lloyd and Mickey are all going home. And, of course, the Chief of Staff.

On these occasions it's traditional to provide a sentimental present, such as a plaque or a framed replica unit flag, to eventually go on the recipient's "love me" wall of their office. Of course, we also do gag gifts, one of which was my contribution of a fake Sandpaper magazine cover. I think it went over better than the custom-made CoS bobble head.

The Army also does urinalysis, regardless of where we are. This is another one of those things that 99% of soldiers agree with on principal but find themselves just a little annoyed when the process is applied to THEM. The U.S. Army takes samples of urine in order to test for drugs. This is done on a random basis most of the time.

The problem is that a lot of people can't "go" on command and some even find themselves inhibited when placed in situation where they have to produce a sample... something like stage fright.

When we're not peeing for Uncle Sam we can join our fellow peacekeepers at the library. Not a huge library, and certainly not a branch of the Great Library of Alexandria, but it had a lot in the way of materials. The emphasis is, of course, on Egypt in general and the Sinai specifically, although

**VIDEOS**

books on the contingent countries are also prominent. I did some more reading on the Arab-Israeli wars as well as local customs and language. Oh, and some P.G. Wodehouse too (it can't ALL be about work!).

I was surprised to discover one day that a book I was reading was listed on the internet as being banned in Egypt... even though I checked it out that week. The Crossing of the Suez, by General Saad el Shazly, is a first-hand account of the 1973 War and was published without the heavy hand of government censorship. Shazly was no fan of the Treaty and I guess his book should have been titled "My Crossing of President Sadat." Shazly found himself in exile even before his book came out.

One of the reasons the Egyptian government didn't like the Crossing of the Suez is because it exposes "military secrets." If poor decisions and bad policy can be described as military secrets then I guess that's true. Americans are lucky that (so far) you can't be placed in jail for criticizing our political leadership or the occasional military bungle.

In the meantime, this pretty much reinforced my self-image of being a badass since I read banned books.

There was a small nook in the library where you can read and drink tea. I would read some of the English-language papers sometimes, seeing what passed for criticism in the Egyptian press ("President Mubarak is just TOO good for us!"). Arab newspapers can have a unique outlook on the news that you don't see in America.

The library also checked out DVDs. There were some oddball films but some pretty solid titles as well. I supplemented the fare available at the library with DVD sets like the complete episodes of Danger Man.

There was a big VHS sale as the library divested themselves of this old technology. I picked up a documentary set about the Beatles, some sci-fi and a video called the Message. This was a video that caused some minor riots when it came out, since it was about the Prophet Mohammed and some Muslims took offense at this.

The Prophet Mohammed is not supposed to be portrayed pictorially. In 1977 the film triggered a hostage situation in Washington D.C. which resulted in future mayor Marion Barry getting a chest wound from a shotgun. The more things change, the more they stay the same.

Anthony Quinn plays Hamza, Mohammed's uncle. It's amazing to me how many ethnicities Anthony Quinn has played in his career. He's played a Basque, a Russian, Greeks, Arabs, and Italians, among others. It's as if whenever a producer needed a character lead he would go find Quinn, whose performance would be identical REGARDLESS of who he was supposed to be. Ironically, this narrow range of acting is what makes him one of my favorite

FMPU

stars. It was a shock for me to arrive in the Middle East and to find that they didn't look anything like Anthony Quinn.

As I said before, I would get videos in the mail, as well as books. Since I have rather eclectic tastes in literature and history my occasional box from home or from Amazon preserved my sanity. Mail was fairly reliable, since we had an Army Post Office at North Camp.

At North Camp the pool is another recreation facility available to its peacekeepers. Officially, the pool is considered an emergency source of water but no one has ever put that to the test that I know of. It was a great way of relaxing, even if the music being played wasn't always the best.

Once we did swimming exercises at the pool for morning PT. Unfortunately the pool was overchlorinated and I wound up with tie-dyed shorts. I looked like an aging hippy and smelled of chlorine the whole day.

AT THE BEAVER LODGE

# 7 CRUISING ON THE RED SEA

Heidi amazed me one day when I spoke to her on the phone. "I've always wanted to visit Egypt!"

This was news to me. Of all the years I've known Heidi, I've never heard her say "Gee, I'd like to visit an overpopulated authoritarian African country." I asked to make sure we were talking about the same thing: "You have?"

"Yes, to see the Pyramids, the Valley of the Kings..."

Then I saw the light. "Oh, you mean THAT Egypt. Well, to get your Egypt you have to go through mine."

The MFO encourages peacekeepers to bring family members over to visit. To that end, there are procedures for asking permission from Rome, Cairo and Tel Aviv, temporary billet requests, etc., etc. But I got them all squared away.

In the meantime I went on another trip to South Camp, this time flying on the new Casa 325. It looks like a mini-Herc, complete with facing seats ("all appendages must be inside the aircraft prior to takeoff"). The French Air Force, for whatever reason, didn't keep their promise to send a replacement Twin Otter.

Down at the beach I completed my Level III WST, almost drowning Captain Buck while "rescuing" him. I had enough trouble keeping myself afloat so pulling Buck along the ride slowed me down while sloshing water over his face. If I learned anything at all from this lesson it was do everyone else a favor: don't help.

Also attended the ITCON medals parade. We drove to the Coastal Patrol Unit facility, located in a nearby harbor. The Italians keep 75 sailors in the Sinai to man their four vessels: the *Esploratore, Sentinella, Vedetta* and *Staffetta*. These vessels are unique, not just for the Italian Navy but for the world, for being "peacekeeping vessels" built specifically for this mission.

The Italian peacekeepers wore their "whites" for the ceremony and the Fijian Band played in their kilts. Afterwards the Italians took us into the Gulf of Aqaba, where we watched dolphins and had refreshments. Good thing we're in the desert or I might get seasick. Everyone had fun and it was nice to meet some civilians, especially British expats.

We even saw some dolphins. Come to think of it, I never saw them

## THE CASA

come up for air. Maybe they were really sharks with good image consultants.

When we returned to the docks we got a really good look at the new billboard the Egyptians put up right outside the fence. The naval facility now had a giant, 30 or 40 foot banner of Mubarak looming above us. It was not a flattering photo. His expression had an odd smile, like you would expect of a villain in a spy movie. "No Mr. Bond; I expect you to die."

Back at North Camp Sporties Bar held dart competitions. I had never played darts before and I found out just how seriously the Kiwis and the Australians take it. Myself, I was happy just to miss the patrons who were enjoying their drinks. I had some fun and managed to score a few points as well. We had several such places where adult beverages could be consumed. Unlike Saudi Arabia there is no prohibition in Egypt so almost every contingent had their own bar. There was once a practice called "Travelling Around the World" in which you would go to each contingent bar and drink the national drink. All I remember is that the Hungarian one was called an AK-47 (made with something called "unicum") and that you shouldn't start from the HUNBAR.

For my own part I found it interesting to work with soldiers from the other side of the old Iron Curtain. Like me, the commander of the HUNCON was a former air defender... only he operated a Soviet surface-to-air missile systems instead of an American one. Ironically he was in the 11th Antiaircraft Brigade of the Hungarian Army when I was in the 11th ADA Brigade of the U.S. Army.

From my conversations with them, it seemed that the majority of soldiers were civilian police drafted into the Hungarian Army specifically to do this job... at the time Hungary didn't have MPs. Hungarians armed with AK-47s (the rifle, not the drink) would provide security aboard the buses running between the camps.

Drinking was one pastime enjoyed by soldiers of just about all the contingents but it rarely got out of hand. However, I do believe that some personnel from Army Central stationed in the Persian Gulf would get themselves invited to join inspection teams or to personally ferry paperclip inventory paperwork for the opportunity to enjoy a beer... since General Order Number One applies while on duty in the Gulf. This order prohibits the drinking of alcohol in theater. It also prohibits pornography, gambling and defacing archeological sites, so spray-painting "Up Yours, Hammurabi" and providing graphic illustration to reinforce it on a ziggurat is definitely *verboten*.

I really didn't understand the ARCENT mindset towards Egypt. Another time the Janan showed up for work looking a little under the weather. "Are you tired?" I asked.

DARTS NIGHT

"Well, the pilot for the general coming over from Kuwait called after midnight." He yawned. "The guy wanted to know if we could make reservations for him at the nearest hotel."

"He WHAT?"

"When I explained to him that there are no hotels in this area he said he could see on the map that we were near an international airport and he found it hard to believe that there are no 5-star hotels near an international airport."

I turned to the map and studied it carefully. Then I asked "Is it possible he was talking about Arafat International Airport?"

Yasser Arafat International Airport is a colossally stupid idea. It is a world-class stupid idea. It is right up there with biological warfare or a Paris Hilton Prize for Literature, it's THAT stupid.

When Israel signed the Oslo II Accords it provided for an international airport in the Gaza Strip. I can't imagine a worse business plan than to operate an airport named after a famous terrorist, run by ex-members of the PLO and serviced by Palestinian Airlines ("Service with a Smile and a Submachine Gun"). Naturally, Israel obliterated it in 2001 when the Gaza Strip started providing a launch pad for terror rockets.

The workers at the ticket counter and the baggage handling areas were still manning their posts up to the year before I got there, ready to confirm that aisle seat or check your carry-on, even though the runway had been rendered unusable.

Long story short, I asked Janan what he did.

"I explained the situation to him and told him they would get VIP quarters here at North Camp."

I shook my head. "If he woke ME up I would have made reservations for him at the Gaza City Hilton. I would have even asked him if he wanted a view of the Mediterranean and the nightly fireworks show." I smiled. "Of course, he'd be disappointed when he got here..."

It wasn't just ARCENT that gave me headaches. Other times, units like 1st Sustainment Command wanted to visit the 1SB, since the sustainment battalion came under the 1st TSC for administrative purposes. Unfortunately, the 1st TSB liked to keep their options open regarding who they sent on visits. Once they waited until the last minute to provide the info on two NCOs, which of course just made our job that much more difficult since we had to get approval via Rome and Cairo.

Had a good time with the CANCON during Canada Day at the Beaver Lodge, the service club they run. The Fijians sang "Oh, Canada," and we had a chance to socialize. The CANCON put on a good spread. I'm not sure what kind of filling was in those meat pies, though. It tasted kind of familiar... could it have

RAFAH

been moose? I hadn't ate like that since Alaska.

We had a few stray cats around the camp. These animals kept the number of rodents down around the area. I nicknamed one of them "Gaza" and he loved me when I had a can of spam.

Once I was practicing my ukulele after hours and Gaza watched me from a distance. I heard the beep of the washer and I put the uke down on the grass. When I came back Gaza was sneaking up on the ukulele... and then gave it a good whack and then ran into the night.

Everybody is a music critic.

Not long afterwards I began to feel ill. I went to the clinic and saw the Hungarian doctor, Captain Nagy. It turned out I was coming down with what is charmingly called the "Sadiqis," a severe form of diarrhea. Everyone comes down with it sooner or later in this part of the world.

I took the medication Nagy prescribed. It wiped me out, left me with no energy. I slept for 17 hours straight.

The Colombians have their national day on July 20th. The day before they carried out their Death March, a very challenging exercise in the 120 degree heat, and a dinner. The dinner, featuring culinary delights from South America, also saw each of us wearing two bamboo cups on cords around our necks.

The Colombians had two drinks to sample in small wooden cups. One tastes like licorice and is supposed to be drunk in one gulp. The other is green and made of pears. I'm hazy on the details after that. I remember a dance in native costume which featured a woman whacking a man with a broom.

Or it might have been some kind of a hallucination left over from my recent bout of the Sadiqis.

Finally it came time for Heidi's visit. I took some leave and she arranged for someone to watch the cats and we both started out for Israel.

My trip to Tel Aviv was uneventful. I had half a day to kill before Heidi's plane arrived at 0020 hours. I spent the time walking around the streets, looking at the occasional pedestal and its plaque. Stories from the birth of modern Israel are immortalized on these plaques: one site states that British officers were captured and held hostage by the Irgun. Another described how signal lamps were lit in order to guide immigrants to the beach. Yet another talked about "Shop A," where the Hagenah had an illicit arsenal.

The Israelis didn't mess around. Just about every block had one of these helpful history markers in English and Hebrew.

I stopped at the McDonald's near the beach for lunch and allowed

TEL AVIV

myself to be inspected by the guard, then went over and tried to pick something out of the menu above the servers. Then I noticed that there was another guy also looking over the menu.

I don't know how I didn't see him before... all he was wearing was swimming trunks and a rifle.

I looked back at the guard, but he didn't seem very concerned. Another look at the weapon confirmed it was a .303 Lee-Enfield. It turned out that the man was a lifeguard. They carry rifles because of the occasional attempt by islamoterrorists to infiltrate by rubber raft. From what I was told, the terrorists teach their men how to inflate the raft and operate the motor but not how to swim... it's only necessary to put a hole in the raft to put an end to the attack.

Or it could have been that the lifeguard just carried them to deal with sharks. They're a dangerous nuisance too.

I got to the airport on time but Heidi's plane came in late. It was a couple hours into the next morning before we were together again.

We were about to leave from the taxi stand when someone stopped us. "Are you Americans?"

"Yes, why?"

He gestured to a young lady nearby. "Could you take this woman to her hostel? She doesn't have taxi fare."

I shrugged. "Sure. I hate the idea of someone being stranded in a foreign country."

I told the girl to get in up front and give the address to the driver. Heidi and I got in the back.

Heidi and I were talking, getting caught up on things, when I looked out the window and something didn't seem right. I leaned forward to talk to the driver. "Hey, this isn't Jaffa, is it?"

"Yafo?" The guy responded. "Yes. Yafo!"

"Great." I muttered under my breath.

"What's wrong?" Heidi asked.

"I'm not ALLOWED to be in Jaffa." I told Heidi. MFO peacekeepers were prohibited from visiting the area, probably because of the curfew in effect there and the occasional problems created by some of the Arab residents. But we dropped off the young lady and went back to our own hotel with no problem. Why the young lady wanted to go to a hostel in Jaffa I'll never know.

The next morning we went to a buffet breakfast with an excellent view of the sea. We walked around a bit on the beach but the heat was too much for Heidi. We went back to the hotel and relaxed a bit until our bus left at 1200.

Our trip from Tel Aviv to Be'ersheva was pretty uneventful. It was an eye-opener to Heidi though, as some Israeli reservists (some of them female)

BE'ERSHEVA

were eating lunch at an outdoor café… and were leaning their Galil rifles against the chairs as they ate. THAT's the kind of thing that cuts down on "lone wolf attacks."

Once at the border we ran into a few problems on the Israeli side, since we were missing a form. On the Egyptian side we had to wait for the customs inspector, an edlerly man who looked old enough to have gone through Allenby's bags when he landed during the Great War. I wonder if Allenby had any risqué French postcards showing an ankle or two…

At OP 1J we stopped and waited near the southern corner of the Gaza Strip for our escort to show up. Once the white MFO vehicles showed up everyone was required to don body armor. This was just a precaution but one that was an eye-opener to the civilians on the bus, Heidi included.

It didn't help that the escorts told us we would be going to North Camp via a roundabout route. It seemed that there were some Bedo protests in Rafah involving some burning tires in the road. Just to top off the day the Israelis conducted an airstrike somewhere in Gaza.

The next day we had some time to relax and I showed Heidi around the camp. Not much going on other than some Congressional staffers, and we stayed out of their way. She met a few of the people I work with and later we watched TV over in the Visitor Quarters. We had some good laughs. Later she helped me try to reconstruct what was in my missing crate so I could put in a claim.

We departed on the next bus to Cairo. Unfortunately, we made a wrong turn and wound up in Rafah on market day. Even though we were in a sightseeing bus I seriously doubt anyone thought we were on a special tour of disaster areas of the Middle East. Peeking through the window curtains we could see the faces of the crowd, some curious but others hostile.

Once we were clear of town and our police escort got clear of the mob we made good time. Heidi videotaped of some of the sights and the interesting people along the route to Qantara, our rest stop. I took a photo of her in the small restaurant where you can stock up on snacks and drinks and didn't realize until later that I got a picture of her with a giant photo of Yasser Arafat leering at her.

There isn't much to see at Qantara itself, or at least not in the area we stopped in. One of the few things worth photographing was an old, beat-up sign nearby which said "UN Peacekeepers Welcome." I guess we inherited the place from UNEF.

We crossed the Suez Canal and were duly warned not to take photos "for security reasons." As if you can't get on the internet and find hundreds of

CAIRO MUSEUM

pictures of the Canal and the Peace Bridge, including satellite photos. It reflects the military mentality which drives this part of the world I suppose.

We checked into the Mövenpick with no trouble (I was smart enough to make reservations this time) and had a buffet lunch. Later our tour group picked us up and we drove to the Nile, passing the Citadel, the City of the Dead and several statues of the royal dynasty overthrown by the Army in 1952.

We took a riverboat tour of the city, part of the package Heidi arranged for us before she left the States. We had dinner and then the entertainment began. First there were the Nubian dancers, who grabbed members of the audience to join them (Heidi and myself included). We had fun, clapping and dancing around the tables. Then a belly dancer came out and started doing this undulating thing with her midriff. She also put a riding crop on my head and balanced it there. I don't know why.

Next were some stick dancers, a traditional in some parts of Egypt. The sticks in question are shepherd staffs covered by colorful Bedo cloth. This was followed by some Dervishes, who did some tricks involving centrifugal force and their colorful skirts, which can be removed and spun in all sorts of ways. I wanted to get a good picture and I turned to Heidi to get the camera. When I turned back one of the dervishes was right next to me and casually said "Hello! How are you doing?" The skirt was spinning over our heads.

It was a fun night!

Fijian sergeant-major inspecting band members at their drill
field (notice the leather wrist-band). Fiji has contributed to a
number of peacekeeping forces and has earned a reputation for
reliability and professionalism. Bainimarama, the prime minister
of Fiji at the time, was once an MFO peacekeeper.

# 8        VALLEY OF THE KINGS

The next day we slept in late, then made our way to the Egyptian Museum. As we got in the taxi the driver asked "Are you Americans?"

"Yes, we are."

"You like President Bush?"

"Sure." I responded. Hey, I'm no commie.

He made a face. "We don't like Mubarak."

"Yeah, I've heard that." I said absent-mindedly.

Heidi leaned close to me. "Don't agree with him. We could get in trouble."

"Heidi, this is Egypt. Everyone starts a conversation by talking about how much they dislike Mubarak. Saying 'I hate Mubarak' in Egypt is like saying 'Aloha' in Hawaii."

We indeed heard the whole litany about Mubarak, his robbery of Egypt, how he planned on making his son president when he finally stepped down, his poor choice of condiments, etc. but I don't think this entirely minimized Heidi's concern that this guy was working for the State Security Investigations Service.

Traffic in Cairo is interesting. You see things you can't believe are real, much less legal, on the road. I once saw an improvised bus which consisted of a pickup truck with facing seats inside the bed shelter and handles and steps on the outside. At least eight people could ride on the outside of this small truck, holding on for dear life. All I could think of was how fatal it would be for a handle to break off in traffic.

Anyone interested in ancient Egypt has seen photos of the large pink building which houses the Egypt Museum. The museum is a treasure trove of artifacts, dating from the Narmer Palette to Roman busts. For the first time we saw the Tourist Police with their special armbands.

This being July it was extremely hot. We were looking forward to getting inside and enjoying the air conditioning... except that there WASN'T any air conditioning, as they informed us when we were paying for our tickets. Then they asked if we wanted to pay extra to visit the Mummy Room.

"We have Ramses II in there." Said the ticket girl helpfully added.

"I don't care who we have to share the place with, I just want to know if it's air conditioned."

CULTURE!

"Oh yes."

"Then give me two tickets."

I would have found it interesting even if I was by myself but Heidi really knows her ancient history. She told me about the ancient dynasties, the great pharaohs, the significance of the different Egyptian gods and the various objects found in tombs.

We made our way upstairs where the King Tut exhibit is. Most of the burial goods are on display, including the furniture, wooden shrines and the iconic gold burial mask. There was also a statue of Akhenaten, the heretic pharaoh who started his own sun-worship religion. Akhenaten has history's first documented beer belly.

In fact there are so many one-of-a-kind artifacts in the museum that it's impossible not to be impressed. Some objects are known around the world and the world certainly travels to Cairo to see for itself the treasures of ancient Egypt. I overheard people speaking Korean, Spanish, Russian, Japanese and French.

Not only was it hot but we had to leave behind our cameras (photography is forbidden in the museum) and the exhibits lack interpretive signs or plaques (the museum REALLY wants you to buy their guide books). Did I mention it was hot? I've never sweated so much in a museum.

We went into the Mummy Room, which must have been at least 40 degrees cooler than the rest of the museum. Several unmapped mummies lie in state, their skin black and stretched thin over their boney bodies. Once they had the power of life and death over hundreds of thousands of men and women and now they lie on display for tourists to gawk at.

Hatshepsut, the female pharaoh whose mummy was recently identified, was on display. Seti I and Ramses II were there as well and they were supposed to have known Moses personally. What did their lifeless eyes once see all those thousands of years ago?

We went to a snack bar outside the main entrance. They sold, no kidding, Tutburgers, proving the great philosopher Steve Martin's old adage, "He gave his life, for tourism."

We shopped around a little at the Hilton across the street from the museum and had an excellent tea there. We looked at some antiques as well as some of the more modern souvenirs. There was a lovely statue of Cleopatra... I knew it was Cleopatra because it looked just like Elizabeth Taylor. Then we headed back to the Mövenpick in a taxi, passing the 1973 October War Panorama. Then our taxi stalled out in traffic.

This was very bad news. Traffic in Cairo is bad enough without becoming an obstacle. We were near a major intersection and the traffic cop

102

CYCLORAMA

was getting frustrated with us. Finally, after some praying (or cajoling) the taxi started back up and got us to the safety of the hotel.

While waiting in the lobby of the Mövenpick we saw a wedding party. The video cameras were huge, like they must have used some two- or three-inch tape format. I've seen shoulder-fired antitank guided missiles less bulky than this thing. Also they were trailing a huge cable that I was sure was going to be tripped over by the wedding party any moment... either this thing was providing a live feed to a television setup somewhere else in the Hotel or that thing used more power than a small radar.

Our next adventure was an early-morning flight on EgyptAir to Luxor. First of all, there was no line to board the plane... just a mob. And it was every man and woman for themselves to get on the plane.

Once we were at Luxor we waded through another crowd at the Arrivals Terminal, looking for the driver that the travel agency arranged for us. In small knots the crowd dispersed and we soon found ourselves alone in the airport with security guards eyeballing us. After several frantic calls on Heidi's cellphone we learned that our driver was delayed enroute to the airport, something about a military convoy hogging up the road.

Yasser, our guide, picked us up and drove us toward Luxor. We passed between several pairs of sphinxes, giant rams facing each other. It was like something out of the movie The Ten Commandments and I almost expected a chariot to drive down the other side of the road. These statues had only recently been excavated and I suppose the road was rerouted to take advantage of this new find.

Luxor sits on the site of ancient Thebes, once the capital of Egypt and the home of the pharaohs. During its glory days the city's great temples and palaces were built to commemorate the achievements of the God-Kings and to awe the masses. Thebes was also the gateway to the Valley of the Kings.

We went to the west bank (the "dead" side) of the Nile. We stopped at the twin Colossi of Memnon. Photos of the statues don't do them justice. They used to make some sort of a whistling or moaning sound up to a hundred years ago or so, when an earthquake put an end to that.

We took some pictures. I didn't want to complain at the time but there was some kind of rodent the size of Gaza... the cat, not the strip.

We passed near the Ramesseum, a temple built to honor and remember Ramses II. This would have been an awesome site to visit on its own merits but there is so much more to see on the West Bank. Heidi pointed out the small house on a hill overlooking the entrance to the Valley of the Kings. She recognized the building as one occupied by Howard Carter, the archeologist who discovered King Tut's tomb in 1922.

104

Heidi at Luxor. The pharoahs tried to build their temples to overawe the peasants... and they succeeded. The scale and the beauty of Egyptian art must have seemed unworldly to the common laborer or farmer.

We were soon at the visitor's center, a nice modern facility built by the Japanese. I was really impressed by the three-dimensional representation of the tombs and their entrances and their proximity to each other. It reminded me of an ant colony. The center listed which tombs are currently open to visitors... some tombs remain closed for years in order to minimize the environmental impact of tourists trudging in and out of the ancient edifices. Additionally, each visitor is permitted to enter three tombs per trip.

We first went to the tomb of Ramses IV. He was the third pharaoh of the 20th Dynasty and was a builder. His tomb was finished "on time," that is before the pharaoh's death, so all it decorations and writings were complete when he was buried in it. And the artwork is impressive, looking as if it had been done last week. The only thing that marred the hieroglyphs were the later Greek and Roman graffiti written during a much later age. I guess Alexandopooloo and Burkus Crassus just had no respect for Egyptian culture.

Next we traveled past King Tut's tomb, the only tomb in the Valley of the Kings which is still occupied by a mummy, has its own air conditioning and costs an extra 80 Egyptian pounds to enter. We passed on entering it as we expected a line there.

We went to Siptah's tomb. He was a pharaoh of the 19th Dynasty and in his case the pharaoh expired before the contract on his burial place was fulfilled. The main corridor was rough; the teams of workers who would have smoothed out the walls and painted the murals depicting the glories of and victories of the God-King Siptah never got their chance to decorate the place.

The last tomb we visited was that of Thutmose III. The sixth pharaoh of the 18th Dynasty, Thutmose has been called "the Napoleon of Ancient Egypt." To get to his tomb we had to climb up a set of metal stairs to where the entrance was hidden in a small ravine. Thutmose went to a lot of trouble to hide his final resting place from would-be grave robbers.

Once inside there were more surprises. At the bottom of the first ramp was a pit. I wonder if any tomb raiders wound up at the bottom of that trap, inadvertantly adding themselves to the archeological record.

Thutmose III also died before his tomb was done but his was further along than Siptah's. The pictoglyphs looked like cartoon stick figures instead of full figures, but the various gods and royals were recognizable. Von Daniken might have written about these ancient "comic strips of the gods" if he ever actually saw them. I wonder if the ancient Egyptians drew the stick figures first and then went over them again later to make them full figures.

Unlike the other tombs, this one was HOT. Instead of being in the valley floor the tomb was actually inside a mountain peak and I think the heat might have been radiating inwards from the surface.

I could feel myself sweat. The caretaker (or maybe he was just an old

THE OLD, OLD, *OLD* ARMY!

guy who likes hanging out in tombs) offered to let us stick our hands in the stone sarcophagus for a pound. We passed on the opportunity... maybe I saw too many mummy movies as a kid to take a chance that there wouldn't be some bandaged hand grabbing me and pulling me in there with it. Or maybe I'm just reluctant to mess with antiquities.

Next our guide brought us to Hatshepsut's Temple. Hatshepsut was a rarity in Egyptian history: a female pharaoh. She ruled over Egypt while wearing a fake beard and seemed to be unusually competent, for someone who ruled in an absolutist theocratic hereditary state. Interestingly, she was succeeded by Thutmose III, the same Thutmose whose tomb we visited.

There is some argument in archeological circles as to whether Hatshepsut and Thutmose got along with one another. Hatshepsut almost certainly kept Thutmose on the sidelines even though his claim to the throne was much stronger than hers. And there seems to be evidence that some years after her death an attempt was made to "erase" her from history by eliminating her name and likeness from official monuments which served in those days as government records.

The statues of Hatshepsut standing in front of the columns are recently restored; most of them were found broken up and dumped in a pit. On the walls there are paintings of various military campaigns and trading expeditions, including one to the land of Punt.

As we left we had to run the gauntlet of souvenir *wallahs* selling their wares on the route between the Temple and the parking lot.

One guy came up to me holding three fist-sized busts of some pharaohs. "Fifteen! Only fifteen!"

Even though I wasn't really looking for anything for myself I thought that deal wasn't bad and they might make good presents for friends. "Fifteen pounds?" I said as I took out Egyptian money, "Sure. I'll do that."

"No, fifteen *dollars*."

I put my money back. "You're out of your mind."

Next we recrossed the river and went to the Temple at Karnak. This was probably the largest religious complex in the world when it was constructed and it must have made the common people feel pretty insignificant when they stood there during ceremonies. Stories in the form of hieroglyphs cover most of the columns and there are small nooks and crannies to explore. Heidi took a picture of me in front of a "scoreboard" which listed all the cities conquered by Thutmose III.

We had seen and done a lot and much of it outside in 120 degree heat. We were wiped out. Back at the hotel the tour company had arranged a courtesy room for us to use while we waited for our nighttime flight back to

# DRAWINGS

Cairo.

I didn't understand the concept of the "courtesy room" until I spent the day hiking around the Valley of the Kings. Having a nice, comfortable air-conditioned room is a blessing after being in Luxor off-season. We cleaned ourselves up and went down to the bar, which sits facing the Nile and the Valley of the Kings on the far side. A single *dhow* sailed up the river while we sat drinking Coca-Cola.

"This must have been what it looked like all those thousands of years ago." Heidi sighed, taking it all in.

I couldn't do anything but agree with her.

We went back to the room. A balcony overlooked the main lobby area and a show started downstairs. We went out to watch the dervishes and other entertainers perform.

Then we decided to leave, since our tour guide would be arriving shortly to take us to the airport. I turned to the sliding door... and it wouldn't open. It was locked! There was a sticker on the door in English and Arabic. It stated that the door locked automatically when closed.

Who the heck designs their hotel so the balcony locks behind the guests?! It was like something out of nightmare or a Pink Panther movie. We tried to catch the attention of someone in the lobby below but there was too much noise and everyone was watching the show. We were yelling but we couldn't be heard over the entertainers.

Fortunately the door to the balcony next to us opened up and a young female Japanese tourist came outside. She didn't speak a word of English but somehow, through pantomime and gestures, we were able to convey the need to get the desk clerk up to our room and open the door.

We got to the airport in time for our flight as well as an opportunity to be eyeballed by an Egyptian colonel who was waiting in the main hall. Maybe Heidi was right to be concerned about the secret police.

The next leg of our journey was to head to Sharm. We were the only ones on the MFO bus making the run from Cairo to Sharm el-Sheikh. Heidi took the opportunity to rest on the bus since she wasn't feeling well and there wasn't much to see once we cleared the tunnel under the Canal. On arrival we got set up in temporary billets and relaxed on Herb's Beach. Heidi and I snorkeled on the reef for a bit and found a spot to get some sun.

"Don't look, Heidi!" I tried to warn her but it was too late: she already got a look at Herb wearing a leather speedo as he made his way to the chinup bar. I know that for myself the mental image of Herb hanging upside down wearing nothing but a leather pouch will haunt me forever.

We did typical tourist things in Sharm: we had a milkshake at the Hard

OFFICE CALL

Rock Cafe and looked for various souvenirs in the local *suq*. They had big soapstone statues standing three feet high of Anubis, duplicates of ones found in Tut's tomb. Unfortunately, shipping and handling would have made them prohibitively expensive to get home.

Another long bus ride, this time back to North Camp. I got sucked into some more work and was in my office on Heidi's last night at the camp when I heard music from outside.

I turned and looked at her: "Is that 'Sway' by Bobby Rydell?"

We were delighted to find an Egyptian band entertaining the peacekeepers at the stone stage. They were pretty good and played some great songs. You haven't lived until you've listened to an Egyptian band playing "Delilah" by Tom Jones. Having drunk Australians singing along with the band made it even more memorable.

On the return trip to Tel Aviv we got stopped at the border. A line of buses carrying Palestinian refugees were waiting to go to Israel then cross into Gaza. Our bus was directed to the front of the line where a large group of very unhappy Palestinian men were collected.

An Egyptian officer came on board and said that anyone who did not have an ARE ID card had to go to his office nearby with their passports. This little group included Heidi, the outgoing Colombian dentist and two other Columbian officers... coincidentally, all female. I went with them since I wasn't about to leave Heidi's fate in the hands of some Egyptian bureaucrat.

The crowd was very hostile but being held back by Egyptian guards. This situation was probably the scariest one I was in while serving in the MFO. The officer stamped the passports and then we got to run the gauntlet all over again. I was certain that any minute a riot was going to break out.

Once back at Tel Aviv we walked around a bit. Our walking tour included a shop specializing in Bauhaus and a trip by the Bela Lugosi Cafe. You have to admire a restaurant that has the courage to be named after a bloodsucker. But soon it was time for Heidi to go home. Another departure and another hard goodbye to my wife and best friend.

It was back to work, especially on the magazine. In trying to make it as relevant as possible to all the different contingents (and NOT just the TF Sinai folks) I tried different things, like drawing cartoons which required no captions or dialog boxes, calendars showing events and holidays of specific interest to each contingent and articles addressing the MFO as a whole.

I went down to South Camp soon after Heidi's departure, flying down on the CASA. I did my water survival training at the beach and played the ukulele a bit. Lt. Masood, my new Canadian deputy, was working out very well

DESERT SOUVENIRS

although not totally familiar with the issues involving the press. Over the next several months he would prove to be extremely reliable and steadfast in his job.

It was at about this time that we ran into a problem with the brand-new, state-of-the-art x-ray machines purchased for security at the front gate of South Camp. These machines were similar to ones used for airport security and were computerized so when it scanned a bag it provided an enhanced image on the monitor for the screener.

But the machines had other features as well... like a training mode. When an object was fed through via the conveyer belt a stored computer image would be displayed instead of the actual object being fed into the machine. The machines at South Camp were in training mode for weeks before someone noticed.

In other words, when a duffel bag was fed into one end of the machine the computer might show a suitcase. Or when a rucksack was put on the conveyer belt it might appear as an overnight bag. Far scarier than the fact that screeners didn't detect this incongruity right away was the fact that while the machine was in training mode it was displaying objects within the suitcases and overnight bags that the screener might want to be concerned about... such as pistols, hand grenades and Acme Brand beheading swords. And none of these objects were noticed by the screeners.

General Ludvigsen pins MFO medals on members of the Norwegian Contingent at North Camp. The Norwegians had their quirks (such as skiing on dry land) but they filled a vital part of the Force, working important administrative roles. General Ludvigsen himself seemed ideal for the role of diplomat-warrior.

# 9  STRANGE DAYS

In August we had another unfortunate loss of life. This time it was an American soldier driving a truck along the Sharm el Sheikh-Taba Road. As noted before, this road winds quite a bit. There are cliff faces, occasional rock falls and narrow shoulders in spots.

Johnson and another soldier were driving a supply run for USBATT Observation Posts along a particularly dangerous curve when their brakes failed. Both soldiers bailed out of their respective sides of the cab before the truck crashed. The assistant driver was airlifted to Israel for emergency treatment but Johnson did not survive.

I set a goal of 30 minutes to get an initial press release out on the accident but got it in 35. I worked on follow-up releases in the afternoon and waited for queries but none came. No media outlet picked up the story. I suppose it was not colorful enough for the mainstream media.

The memorial ceremony was a few days later at the movie theater. Brigadier General Leonard, the 1st TSC commander, came over on short notice to pay his respects. Although not as elaborate as the Twin Otter ceremony we nevertheless had good representation among the different contingents.

Later the general was flown down to the area where the accident took place and then on to South Camp. The support requirements for the ceremony kept me busy and once the ceremony was done I finally had the rest of the day off. I felt exhausted and perhaps a bit depressed. That made a total of ten peacekeeper names added to the Arch this year.

Almost immediately something came up that lifted my spirits. It wasn't my missing crate, although I still had a forlorn hope that it might arrive after all. Actually, it was what happened at the morning brief.

I went into the staff meeting same as I always do. The slide presentation began not with the normal information brief but with a picture of one of the tiny pickup trucks, its rear end wheels on the 4-foot high stone stage and the front end smashed on the ground. In the middle of the stage was a golf cart, just sitting there. I thought I heard a couple of chuckles and I might have laughed too if I had gotten more sleep and my brain wasn't shifting gears, trying to figure out what I was looking at.

## ASKING FOR DIRECTIONS

Just to set the stage for the reader (so to speak), the stone stage is where we put on shows. It's pretty much just a stone platform built higher than the rest of the little plaza adjacent to the Force Exchange. The only way up and down are by narrow stone stairs on either side, which made me wonder how the golf cart and at least part of a pickup truck got up there...

But my reverie was broken by the sound of the Force Commander's voice saying "That is NOT FUNNY! This is not acceptable! We are NOT university students!"

General Ludvigsen was genuinely upset. For a moment I thought he was going to go all Viking on us and bring out a broadsword or something.

Once everyone composed themselves we got the full story: the night before a group of Aussies and Kiwis were enjoying themselves at one of the clubs and when the festivities ended they staggered back towards their billets. As they passed the stage one of them saw the golf cart belonging to the detested Physical Instructor. "Hey mates! Do you know what would be brilliant? What if we were to put the PI's cart up on the stage?"

Everyone agreed that this would indeed be brilliant and that there were enough of them to lift the machine up on the stage. After a few minutes of boozy grunting the deed was done. They were congratulating themselves on this practical joke when someone else said "You know what would be even MORE brilliant? What if we put the truck up on the stage?"

Everyone looked at the nearby truck and agreed that this was an even better idea than the first one. Now, the pickups employed by the MFO are much smaller than anything on U.S. roads but looks can be deceiving. In this case, it was relatively easy to lift the rear end of the truck onto the stage but the front, where the cab and the small engine were, turned out to be a bit TOO heavy. Not only could they not get it on the stage but the gang from Down Under managed to drop it from two or three feet off the ground, damaging the front of the machine.

That's when I discovered that many of the white trucks with the MFO emblem don't actually BELONG to the MFO... they're leased. Now the MFO was on the hook for the damage done.

From a legal and disciplinary point of view the Force Commander has no authority based upon the military codes of the various contingents. In the case of a U.S. soldier, for instance, Ludvigsen had no authority to inflict non-judicial punishment in accordance with the Uniform Code of Military Justice. In fact, the Force Commander has only one tool available to him... he can point to any peacekeeper and state "YOU are no longer a member of the MFO." That person must now depart the Sinai and return to his or her national control.

HAKA DANCE

This is done sparingly since, regardless of which contingent you belong to, failure to complete your tour of duty due to a disciplinary infraction is NOT going to help your military career. And this is what we were looking at for both the New Zealanders and the Australians involved in this party joke gone horribly wrong. Funny, but horribly wrong.

Both contingent commanders went to the Force Commander to try to cut a deal with him. Understanding the need for good order and discipline they offered to provide appropriate punishments to the people involved but my understanding was that Ludvigsen still wanted to make an example of the senior person present, an Australian. In fact, he wanted him gone.

A compromise was worked out. The Australian only had a few more months before his tour of duty in the Sinai was over. Instead of sending him home, he was sent to a Colombian OP for the remainder of his tour.

We were discussing the misfortune of our fellow staff officer at the dining facility when some asked "Does he even speak Spanish?"

"After three months with no one to talk to but a half-dozen Colombians?" I gave a small laugh. "If he doesn't know the language now he will by the time he gets back."

The Australians have a historical link to the region. In WWI it was the Australian Light Horse which distinguished itself at the battles of Gaza and Be'ersheva. In WWII it was Australian soldiers of the British Army which helped defeat Rommel in North Africa, especially at El Alamein.

The AUSCON soldiers make an annual pilgrimage to El Alamein to commemorate that critical battle and Australia's role in it. In 1942 the battle saw the Axis forces overextended but virtually at the Nile delta. Commonwealth forces, including Indian and Australian units, smashed the Germans and Italians and started an Axis retreat that wouldn't end until they were well outside Egypt's borders.

Egypt's role in the war was odd. Cairo broke off relations with the Axis soon after the war began in North Africa. However, Egypt was technically neutral right up to the end of the war, even when U-boats sank Egyptian shipping and the war raged back and Axis troops invaded Egyptian territory.

The role of the Egyptian Army largely consisted of plotting against the British and creating "Willkomen Rommel" banners to drape across the streets of Cairo to greet the Afrika Korps. Sadat himself was placed in prison for being part of such a conspiracy.

I was sorry that I wasn't able to go with the Australians to see the battlefield. Many tanks and guns have been collected at the impressive war memorials there. A lot of Germans, Italians, English, Indians and Australians are buried at El Alamein.

Italian crew piping TF Sinai commander aboard.

One of the Italian patrol ships in the Red Sea. Sharm el-Sheikh
is in the distance.

We got in a new U.S. Chief of Support, a pretty nice guy. Colonel Scott M. Carlson, a recent War College graduate, immediately got down to business and fit right in to the daily routine of the Sinai. I don't think anyone disliked him.

Not long afterwards we had a visit from 1st TSC that flew in, which seemed pretty routine until I got a call from the Force Commander.

"James, who is leaving on the flight this afternoon?" he asked. I thought this was odd, since he already knew who the official party was.

"Sir, as far as I know it will just be the U.S. one-star, his aide and the aircrew."

"I want you to check on that and let me know." And he hung up.

I looked at the time. The plane was scheduled to leave shortly. I called the Flight Following section and was told that as far as they knew it was the same people who came in and that's what I reported.

But in fact the plane left ahead of time and with Colonel Carlson on board. At first I thought he must have had a family emergency and 1st TSC flew him to Kuwait to get him on a Rotator flight to the States, circumventing all the red tape involved in getting him out from Cairo or Tel Aviv. Highly irregular, but not outside the realm of possibility. Then we were told through Task Force Sinai that he would not be coming back, not for his personal gear or the stuff in his office. To say the least this was very odd.

The next day I did a media sweep on the internet, which was part of my routine, and came across a story in the Army Times. Colonel Carlson had been involved in some sort of a conspiracy in which he swapped places with another War College student in an effort to "disprove" his paternity in an ongoing case in which he was accused of fathering a child with one of the soldiers in a unit he previously commanded.

Colonel Carlson's picture was on the cover of the Army Times.

I was absolutely livid. I had been made to look as if I lied to Ludvigsen (although he never spoke to me about it) and worse, I would have been caught completely flat-footed if the Army Times had called me in the Sinai to confirm details of Carlson's service in the Sinai.

It soon became clear that senior leadership knew about Carlson's situation but left me out of the loop. Things like that made me feel like I wasn't quite part of the team. Did someone really think I was going to call CNN with this ground-breaking story?

I went on the air on our radio station for the first and only time. I wanted to make sure I knew the procedure for switching off the automated system and cutting in with a live feed. I should have done a better job of reading the script ahead of time but I managed to fumble through it. My DJ career as "Jimmy Sinai" ended the same day it began.

AUSSIE

At about this time there was a half-hearted Hamas attack in the Fijian sector. A single mortar shell fell near OP 1J and three others "walked" across the fence towards Kareem Shalom, a nearby Israeli settlement. This was the second mortar attack near the Gaza corner in the last couple of months. This time, however, a couple of men were seen speaking on cellphones, apparently giving fire direction. Good thing Israel allows PalTel to provide cellphone service in Gaza.

We suspected at the time that the Egyptian security forces would simply dismiss attack as having been caused by rifle fire, despite the shattered concrete at OP 1J. The Egyptians did not want to admit that the situation was escalating beyond their control near Gaza.

There was another crazy incident at about this time. I received a call at the office from someone who said he was a colonel reporting for duty at the U.S. Embassy in Cairo.

I was a bit confused by this. "Well, how can I help you, Sir?"

"I'm at the airport." He said. "There are two guys in civilian clothes who claim they're supposed to report to the MFO."

I started laughing. "That's not possible. The U.S. doesn't bring in replacements via Cairo and we're not expecting anyone." Then a disturbing thought came to mind. "Did they say what their job specialty is?"

"Aircraft fuel handler."

Uh-Oh. It was just possible...

"So what exactly is going on there?" I asked.

"They're trying to get past immigration with their orders. The police seem to be getting pretty aggravated with that."

It was very fortunate that the colonel happened to be going through the airport at the same time as these two soldiers and that he had a working cellphone. It was also very fortunate that the colonel took the time to try to help rather than just take the attitude that it "wasn't his problem."

"Sir, can I please talk to one of the soldiers?"

The colonel handed me off to one of them. I told him who I was. He explained to me that he and the other private had been in the fuel handlers course just the previous week. An officer entered their classroom and informed them that they would be joining the MFO right after graduation, no ifs, ands or buts.

Now I understood why the situation had developed the way it had. We were desperately short of fuel handlers for the Blackhawk helicopters and we sent a message through channels that if replacements were not sent ASAP we would shortly become non-mission capable.

So, in response to this someone gave orders for the next available

INSTIGATOR

trained fuel handlers to be put on a plane and sent to Cairo. After all, Cairo is in Egypt and the Sinai is in Egypt so it's all the same, right?

Wrong. These soldiers were arriving only with a set of U.S. Army orders, which Egypt is not obligated to recognize. They did not go through the training at the OCONUS Replacement Center, so they had little or no idea what conditions to expect. And they did not have official maroon passports with the necessary visas from the Egyptians. But worst of all, WE DIDN'T KNOW THEY WERE COMING!!!

I told the two soldiers to hold tight and not to let the police take them anywhere. I called the MFO office in Cairo and asked for General Ashraf.

To get anything done in Egypt you have to know a general, either an active-duty one or a retired one. We kind of kept one on retainer. I didn't get to speak to him direct but I gave the details to the person at the office before I left to go to a meeting.

When I came back Jim, my Fijian NCO, told me everything was OK with the two soldiers. "They have been remanded to General Ashraf's custody."

I froze. "Please tell me that isn't the way he put it."

Jim, an extremely efficient NCO, pulled out his notes and read them out loud: "...remanded to custody."

"Oh.... Crap."

"What's the matter?" Mahsood asked.

"They've been *remanded to General Ashraf's custody.* This means that for all practical purposes they are under arrest, they just don't have to go to jail." I breathed deep. "OK, let's start unsnarling this mess."

We were able to get them transport over to North Camp from the MFO-Cairo office and to start the process to get them an "official" passport. Ironically, one of them later broke his ankle and had to be transported across the Egyptian border to Israel, where he was flown out, never officially having been in Egypt as far as the Egyptians were concerned. Oh, and we were able to head off two more soldiers who handed airline tickets, given a pat on the head and pointed in the general direction of the airport.

I was able to get the injured fuel handler over the border with little or no trouble, but that was traveling from Egypt to Israel. From Israel to Egypt was a little more complicated, thanks to Egypt's rigid bureaucracy.

I received a phone call from the border crossing at Nizzam stating that the bus was being held up because an American at the border at an expired visa for Egypt. This problem could be fixed at North Camp, if all other paperwork was correct, but it was matter of getting him to the base.

While one of the Task Force Sinai soldiers waited in my office I unlocked and pulled open a drawer in my desk. I handed the guy a sticker. "Go to the

**WEAPONS
QUALIFICATION**

border crossing. Ask to see the soldier's passport. Stick this in there when the Egyptian border security guy isn't watching."

He looked at the sticker with its beautiful printing and its holographic eagle. "What is this?"

"It's a brand-new, unissued Egyptian tourist visa. I've found that these help a lot when there is a problem getting into the country."

He looked the sticker. "How did you....?"

"Don't ask." In fact, I had spent money out of my own pocket to obtain those visas and it was one of the best deals I had ever made. Not necessarily one of the most LEGAL deals I had ever made, but you can't have everything.

"But the border guard must have looked at the passport already. He'll know that this visa wasn't in there."

"Put it in the back." I shrugged. "He'll assume he made a mistake and let the guy pass."

And that's how it wound up going, more or less. If the General had a fit about a drunken prank involving a golf cart I could only imagine how irritated he would have been if he found out his Press and Visits Officer was smuggling illegals into Egypt.

# THE FORCE SKILLS COMPETITION **10**

It was interesting living in the Holy Land (even though at times it felt as if the Sinai was more of the Holy Suburbs). When living in this part of the Middle East, regardless of your faith, it's hard to ignore the importance of this area in Mankind's spiritual and historical life. In Cairo there is a story that Joseph, Mary and baby Jesus lived there for a time, after Herod's Massacre of the Innocents in Judea. The Land of Goshen, where the captive Israelites lived before the time of Moses, is somewhere west of the old Canal Zone. And of course there is the Red Sea, where Charlton Heston used special effects to save the Hebrews from Yul Brynner. Or something like that.

Since my religious education was a little "iffy" (I still don't get the whole Easter Bunny thing) I went to Bible study on Sundays. We talked mostly about the Book of Exodus and Moses. I admired the chaplain who did our Protestant services... being a Methodist from Catholic Puerto Rico he must have been pretty lonely on the island.

We did an Iftar, or a Ramadan evening meal, and I found out that I was the Official Greeter. We had the Governor of North Sinai, the Mayor of el Arish, General Nagy and several other Egyptian officials come to North Camp, where we did a wonderful dinner. Our guests were also impressed by the entertainments put on by the Kiwis, Colombians and Fijians under the stars.

During the holy month of Ramadan Muslims are not permitted to eat or drink during daylight hours, so the Iftar is the first time they get to eat that day unless they got up before dawn to eat a little something. It would be hard not to enjoy yourself at an Iftar dinner.

Even so, I was on my feet all evening, making sure everything worked out correctly. Yet another opportunity to be in "show business," especially when it came to taking the group photo.

Speaking of Show business, we got another cheerleader visit, this time from the Kansas City Chiefs. I absolutely dreaded this visit after what I went through with the Ben-Gals.

A young U.S. Army captain was sitting with me at dinner, discussing the impending visit. He was oblivious to the fact that most of my female comrades were treating me like a leper, word having got out that there was yet ANOTHER cheerleader visit on the way.

LUNCH

"Wow, it must be great to escort cheerleaders." He said. "I'll bet they're a lot of laughs."

It suddenly dawned on me that this guy was a newbie and had no idea how the previous visit went. So I decided to do what anyone in the Army would do in my place... I decided to take advantage of him.

"So, would YOU like to do the escort mission?" I asked as casually as I could manage.

"Do you think I could?" He asked, with far more enthusiasm than he would have had, if he had only known.

I tried not to smile as I said "Oh, it might take some work but I think we could swing it..."

The KC Chiefs visit wasn't nearly as crazy as the Ben-gals. But still when that captain got done I asked him how things went.

"I never worked so hard in my life!"

The Force Skills Competition kicked off in October. This was an annual event which pitted teams from most of the contingents against each other in physical endurance, marksmanship, medical knowledge and rules of engagement.

The physical portion consisted of an obstacle course at North Camp, which was grueling given the heat of the Sinai and the difficulty of the 14 individual obstacles, such as the Wall and the Swings. Many of the obstacles are simply impossible to negotiate without teamwork and prior planning. Individually, each competitor had a bare minimum equipment requirement as they ran through the course: ID card, ROE card, tactical vest (or other load-bearing rig), a full canteen of water, a field dressing, toggle rope, weapon and ammunition magazines.

It doesn't sound like much stuff, but when you have to crawl on your hands and knees to get through a tunnel or hang from overhead monkey bars it can get pretty rough after a while. It helped that there were a lot of peacekeepers who came out to the course to watch the proceedings, cheer on their teams and enjoy those "agony of defeat" moments for the opposition. The obstacle course turned into the "happeningest place to be" for a while.

The marksmanship part took place at North Camp's small arms range. The small weapons facility saw each contingent engaging paper targets with the standard issue weapon for their country.

The Observation portion was done at an observation tower set on the ground (as opposed to its normal configuration of being set on stilts). Each peacekeeper was presented with a model of ground vehicles and aircraft they might spot in the Sinai, show to them at a distance from the tower.

New Zealand soldier navigating the obstacle course during the
Force Skills Competition (note the flag and kiwi patches). Teams
of men and women from most of the contigents are pitted against
each other during the FSC.

An American soldier clears the barbed wire obstacle. His velcro
patches have presumably been removed to prevent losing them. he
sand just makes this course that much more interesting.

A Colombian soldier displays toughness and determination in dealing with the rope obstacle.

The Medical Knowledge involved the treatment of simulated casualties during a scenario in which an aircraft has crashed in the desert. Not only were casualties supposed to be identified, evaluated and treated but the "crash site" had to be secured and formatted message radioed to HQ for assistance. These skills might mean the difference between life and death.

The Rules of Engagement portion was another scenario, in which the peacekeeper rode in vehicles and saw various scenes which required a decision on their part on how to react: individuals fighting, men waving around weapons, someone attempting to hide near the road... each of these had to be dealt with according to the established ROE.

I took a bunch of still photos and arranged for video coverage. We tried to follow the competitors as they went through the various tests and obstacles. Given the heat this was almost as rough as running the course itself. It was with great relief that I attended the closing ceremony.

Based on the size of the contingent and the points system the USBATT One and USBATT Two teams scored 3rd and 4th Place in the "Major Unit" category (1st and 2nd were won by Fijian teams) but came in 5th and 6th overall placings. The top combined winner? New Zealand's team.

I was feeding another cat I named Spam. One day he acted odd when I came home and called him. Then I saw the crane nearby... the bird had a broken wing and Spam was hanging around as if he was ready to finish it off. I shooed him away and called the vet. After I got off the phone I sat with the bird and waited for the vet. Spam kept his distance.

The bird looked at me with black and yellow eyes, as if he was deep in thought. Of course, for all I knew he was in pain and had no way of expressing himself. In any case, he wasn't going anywhere.

The vet came out and examined the bird. He told me the crane's case was hopeless. I was crestfallen, since I imagined us setting his wing, visiting him at the vet clinic, teaching him tricks and eventually taking him out to return to the sky.

Instead the vet loaded him in his vehicle to take him back to the clinic in order to euthanize him. I felt bad, even though this wasn't a tragedy of my making. In the course of world events it was a small tragedy but for the bird it was the ultimate tragedy.

Of course, crows are an entirely different story.

North Camp had a pretty lively population of the black birds. Seeing Egyptian crows up close can be a little unnerving at first... they want food and water and get very annoyed at people who get in the way of their basic survival needs.

# FUN AND GAMES

I once saw a discarded juice box on the sidewalk once. Before I could throw it away a crow landed, hopped over to it, punched a hole in the box with his beak, lifted it over his head (the box still attached to his beak) and drank it down. The bird discarded the box with a flick of its head and turned to me as if to "Wadda YOU lookin' at?"

The crows would descend on anything edible. They would raid garbage cans in their search for food wrappers and drink containers. Worse than the nuisance they presented to peacekeepers going about their duties, they also had one place they loved to hang out... the main radio antenna, which consisted of a cable between two towers. They would line one end of the cable to the other sometimes, hundreds of them, making the center of the cable sag a bit. This did not help our reception at all.

At a meeting we discussed what we could do to eliminate them.

One senior officer put it simply: "We got guns. Why don't we just shoot them?"

"I'm not sure it would be a good idea to shoot at ANYTHING within the confines of the camp." Replied another. "After all, stray bullets have to go somewhere..." I chimed in and shared my own idea: "I believe there is a chemical we can spray the crows with that will remove the oils their feathers need in order to provide lift." Everyone looked at me blankly. "If they can't fly, eventually they starve to death."

"How is it sprayed?"

"Oh. By crop-duster." That eliminated THAT idea. None of our aircraft could be adapted for this purpose and who knows what we would have got if we tried to contract the job out.

I think eventually we decided to come up with a trap similar to the one used to collect feral cats and other smaller ground animals. Once collected the vet would euthanize them. I'm not sure what kind of bait you use for crow. Juice boxes might work well.

I was given a false hope that my crate might have arrived. I received an email from Supply saying that a large box had been received with the name of another Fort Bragg soldier on it. The thing was, the soldier in question hadn't shipped any unaccompanied baggage.

Both of us went down to the warehouse to sort out the problem. What we discovered was that the box did indeed belong to the other soldier... it was the gear that was supposed to be in storage until he returned from Egypt. If the Army shipped stuff they were supposed to store, is it possible that they stored stuff they were supposed to ship? In that line of thought lies madness.

Later on I dreamed that I found my crate in a secret government

POWER
OUTAGES

warehouse, gathering dust between the Ark of the Covenant and Hitler's brain.

Another Armed Forces Entertainment visit, this one by Hot Molina, a Latin band which does a lot of overseas tours for the troops. What the Polynesian group was to the Fijians, Hot Molina was to the Colombians, the Uruguayans and the Puerto Ricans. They did a couple of shows, playing Salsa, Rumba, and Cha Cha Cha. A great opportunity for folks to get off their seats and do a little dancing.

I tried to get other entertainers, like close-magic guys, but it was pretty much whatever was available on the circuit. I once talked to Weird Al Yankovic about going on a USO tour but that's a whole different story.

Another time I had to catch a flight to Sharm el Sheikh by way of Cairo on the CASA. When I woke up that morning I had a feeling of dread, as if I should avoid this mission in whatever way I could. I hadn't had that feeling since Desert Storm, when I avoided a scud with my name on it.

It began with takeoff... or lack of it. The CASA had to abort its first takeoff (an extremely unpleasant experience for anyone who has ever been through one) and taxi back. Then the aircrew announced that they thought the problem was in the automatic propeller pitch setting and they were going to fix it... by revving the engine up even higher on the *next* attempt to get airborne.

We got into the air this time but we had to take the "long route" into Cairo, which extended our flight time. And once at Cairo we had to wait for clearance to land. We were flying low enough to see individual landmarks, like the Citadel and the City of the Dead. At one point I think I even spotted the Tomb of the Unknown Soldier. You know you're flying too low when you can make out the expressions of surprise on the faces of the people below.

Unbelievably, despite the delays we had already gone through, the Admiral we were picking up and the rest of the party were not at the airport. We had to wait for the LAWIO generals to board the plane. Now it was time to make our way to Sharm.

At Sharm el-Sheikh the two-vehicle convoy which showed up to get us went to South Camp via the "long way" around town. By the time I arrived a convoy with Colonel Gerard and other members of the staff was about to roll out to the CPU for another Iftar, which was the whole purpose of the exercise. I was left behind as I arranged for my billets and a place to stash my gear.

The convoy came back for a second run and I jumped in a vehicle to go the CPU. I got there just as the Iftar was beginning, so I started taking photos and checked Staff Sergeant James, who was running the audiovisual support for the event.

There had been a run-in between James and Commander Caratelli, one of the senior Italian officers in the ITCON. This came to a head when there was a

## BEDOUIN MARKET

delay while the Italians tried to hook up a karaoke system into the AV equipment and it went down to a shouting match between James and Caratelli. Who gets into a shouting match because they can't do "Volare," anyway?

Overall the event went well but I hitched a ride in the ambulance rather deal with Caratelli again.

I had flown from the Israeli border to Cairo, then to the southern tip of the Sinai peninsula, drove the scenic route around Sharm, drove a little further to attend an Iftar and narrowly avoided a fight over karaoke. I was wiped out when I went to bed.

The next morning I got up and shaved and noticed two dots just under my right sideburn. I didn't spend too much time thinking about it because I had a flight to catch at 0700 and had to get back to North Camp for a Bilat that was scheduled for that day.

Everything was set up but by chance the AVCO UH60 sent to pick up the Israelis made better time than expected... and the Egyptian delegation was not there to greet them. This sounds really petty but it's all about protocol... the Sinai is Egyptian territory and if the Israelis are going to visit then Egyptian authorities must be there to welcome them there.

So we stalled getting them off the helicopter. Finally the Egyptians were there to "officially" greet them. Later on I overheard an Egyptian officer tell one of the Israelis "I don't know WHY they didn't let you off the helicopter... you didn't need us here to meet you."

But I knew better... regardless of what the Egyptians told the Israelis if we had moved the IDF party to the Bilat site or even just to the aircraft control office they would have lodged a complaint to MFO-Cairo and I would have never heard the end of it from Rome.

Over the next few days I noticed the two tiny holes near my ear get bigger, join into one sore, and get bigger still. It wasn't until I started getting a fever and noticed that the scab seemed to be getting convex that I started worrying and went to the clinic.

My first trip to the clinic was rather unsatisfactory. Despite the outside temperature I was getting rather chilly. The doctor gave me a cream for my skin. Even though I only applied it to the area around the bite I wound up with acne from the waist up. Now I was feverish, had a hole that was about the size of a dime in the side of my head and had zits over half my body.

During my second visit to the clinic they came to the conclusion that I had an allergic reaction to the cream. The Force Surgeon also determined that the cause of my initial illness was a bug bite in my sleep (probably a spider) which was causing necrosis in the tissue around the bite. The fever was most likely a zoonotic disease, something in the spider's system that was now in MY

SPORTS!

system. He gave antibiotics for the fever, cleaned out the wound really well, and prescribed lots of rest. As luck would have it, we had a three-day holiday anyways, which I spent covered in blankets while I watched TV in my room. About this time I also caught some respiratory bug that was going around. My luck just kept getting better and better.

1SB had a Halloween party. My roommate Claude came as an evil jester. Another friend of mine was dressed as Austin Powers. The librarian was dressed as character from Canterbury Tales. I wore a fez and a smoking jacket like a 1960s jetsetter. Everyone had a blast.

Keeping with the spirit of Halloween I wrote about the Mystery of OP 3-4, the USBATT remote site which saw all personnel vanish without a trace 25 years before. As the story goes, the disappearance was never solved and the site itself was dismantled and the location struck off all MFO maps. To this day, every Halloween, desperate radio calls are heard from OP 3-4.

Of course, it's just another ghost story.

Just when I thought things would be getting back to normal, the Force Commander asked me about the video which was shot for the Force Competition. He was under the impression that the raw video was supposed to be sent to Rome.

In fact, the video was in the possession of Heidi back at home; I had mailed her the video tapes. Since she had the computer and software to process the video and turn it into a finished product, and in fact also had the training necessary from the Atlanta School of Broadcasting, she had agreed to edit it. No one in Rome had contacted me about sending it to them instead.

So now it was a mad scramble to arrange for the material to get to Rome where I guess a production company had been contracted to turn the footage into a motivational video. Heidi didn't even have a chance to do anything with them. I think that's a shame because we never did see the finished product the contractor.

# MOUNT SINAI AND ST. CATHERINE'S **11**

Tensions were running high. Small unidentified aircraft were spotted by peacekeepers around Gaza... presumably Israeli drones. Lots of small arms fire inside Gaza. Zone Delta saw some tank movements on the Israeli side. Tunnels under the wall were being uncovered all the time by Egyptian authorities, who were being unusually efficient in rooting them out. Someone was encouraging the locals to pitch rocks at MFO vehicles and there was even a report of a guy hiding in a manhole near North Camp. There was a feeling in the air that SOMETHING was going to happen but no one seemed to know WHAT.

For Thanksgiving we had a regular American meal, with lots of turkey and fixings. As part of the U.S. Army tradition, everyone wore greens or dress blue uniforms and the officers took turns serving. By now my skin had cleared and I couldn't be mistaken for a pimply teenager anymore. With the unpleasantness going on in Iraq and Afghanistan, not to mention the Clinton wars in the 1990s, there were certainly enough decorations to go around on our nice Union-blue uniforms.

It was fine meal, especially since it was spent with friends and comrades.

There was an accident involving the Uruguayans, but fortunately no serious injuries. Everyone likes the Uruguayans, but they mostly keep to themselves. Until one of their senior generals visited us I didn't realize how many different hotspots have Uruguayan peacekeepers participating. Like Fiji, their country might be small but they do a lot for the greater global community.

In the meantime, the dreaded purge of the stray cats began. Ham and Spam both disappeared, no doubt to be put to sleep by the vet. I felt sorry for them, even though Spam did hurt one of the local birds.

I didn't even know that Hungary had a rank called Bishop-General until I was mostly through my tour in the Sinai. Then I found out that he wanted to visit Saint Catherine's but since I was Visits Officer I got to go with him as his escort. I didn't mind as I figured this might be my last chance to go there. So I got up at 0300 in order to depart at 0400.

The TREU was responsible for getting us there. The Uruguayan driver of our bus claimed that the heater was broken but after an hour of shivering we found out that he just didn't know how to turn it on. We had heat after we passed Taba and settled down, some folks going to sleep and others reading.

SAINT
CATHERINE'S

The driver sipped his *mate* through a silver straw as rolled on to our destination. Mate is the national drink of Uruguay, a kind of tea made from *yerba mate* leaves. Normally drunk from a gourd, the TREU soldiers often used a stainless steel flask with the same kind of straw built in.

It took seven hours to get to St. Catherine's Monastery, built at the base of the actual Mount Sinai, the very place where God gave Moses the Ten Commandments. Or at least the mountain is one of the possible locations... another candidate is in Saudi Arabia. Some American Christians decided to forge some Saudi documents so they could search for the mountain there... an idea which seems colossally stupid to me.

We got to stay for 70 minutes. The place is 1600 years old and an impressive little outpost in this wasteland. The generations of Orthodox priests who have lived here built a place of worship that is also a veritable fortress. Saint Catherine's is an island of Christianity in a sea of Muslims... or, given the small population in the Sinai, a shallow lake. I was impressed by the beautiful icons and books in the place.

There were a lot of tourists in the place, mostly Greeks and Russians driven to the monastery from Sharm el Sheikh. It was so packed that it was a bit hard to get around but I managed to see the Moses Well, the "elevator" which brought food, water and individuals in and out of the monastery in ancient times and the Church of the Holy Transfiguration. There was a descendent of the Burning Bush as well, a quite ordinary looking plant.

I could have gotten some great shots if only I had the new lenses that were in my crate.

I had to get out of the walls of the place... it was too claustrophobic. I walked down the row of souvenir *wallahs* and bought myself a cheap guidebook, a commemorative scarf and few postcards. I reflected on the fact that if this place was in the United States there would be a stand selling "do-it-yourself" Ten Commandment tablets. People would be encouraged to make up their own commandments like "V. Thou Shalt Not Vote Republican" or "XI. Thou Shall Root For No Team Except the Steelers," thus managing to be unfunny AND blasphemous at the same time.

Then it was time to go and face another six hour ride back. We did pass the old airport near Taba. The airport might have been busy at one time or maybe it was built to accommodate a crush of tourists who never came, but now it hosts a collection of airliners in various Middle Eastern and African liveries. I was told that this is a good place to stash aircraft that are in danger of being "repo'd."

The following day was crazy. A Hungarian An-26 landed, bringing Dr. Vidai, the Deputy Minister of Defense. It was an hour late because Cairo Air

Soldiers of HUNCON 6 on parade. Many of these men and women had been civil police before being sent to serve with the FMPU.

A Hungarian AN-26 visits North Camp. Although the HQ got relatively little air traffic directly to the Sinai it amounted to an interesting collection of aircraft.

Traffic Control rerouted the flight.

It was great to get a close look at an An-26. Of course I had seen other Soviet planes, some at the U.S. Air Force Museum and others (like the An-2 "Red Baron") at the "secret squadron" at Biggs Army Airfield. But this one was a working transport and I liked getting some good shots of it, especially since I never got any good shots at one when I was still in ADA.

The media got off the plane first, followed by the Deputy. The Guard of Honor met her on the tarmac and the Force Commander was there as well. The cameramen and reporters followed her as she made the rounds of the camp, got an official photo taken and went to the MDF for a late lunch... which I was specifically asked to join. I guess it's good to know the Bishop-General.

Another day, another visit. A couple of weeks later I waited at the airfield for Commodore Frank Bainimarama, the Interim Prime Minister of Fiji, to arrive.

For "interim prime minister" read "dictator." The previous year Bainimarama overthrew Fiji's constitutional government because it was "corrupt." In fact, one of the main grievances that Bainimarama seemed to have when it came to the government is that they were being too lenient on the plotters who overthrew the government (briefly) in 2000. So, if you think the government is soft on coups then you get rid of that government with a coup?

The bloodless coup caused a few complications for the MFO, however. When planning for the Commodore's visit there was a question as to whether he was visiting as the head of the armed forces or as the Fijian government's chief executive. In fact he was both. It was decided that he would be treated as the head of the military, which did not warrant the honors or attention we would have given him if he was, say, the Prime Minister of Australia or the President of Colombia.

Then there was the ongoing "cold war" between Fiji and its fellow MFO members Australia and New Zealand. Australian politicians in Canberra demanded a "swift return to democracy." Prime Minister Helen Clark of New Zealand placed sanctions on the new Fijian regime. Both countries put into place a travel ban which rather complicated the rotation of peacekeepers. There were rumors that the two countries even considered military intervention in Fiji. Needless to say, I don't recall any Kiwis or Aussies at the ramp waiting for Commodore Bainimarama to arrive.

One of the Australians joked that the Fiji Infantry Regiment is composed of three territorial (or reserve) battalions and three regular battalions. One

## FORCE EXCHANGE

battalion normally does UN peacekeeping and one does MFO peacekeeping but if peace breaks out somewhere and at least two regular battalions are actually in Fiji at one time then a coup automatically overthrows the government.

The Commodore got off the plane wearing his Navy uniform, which kind of surprised me because I thought he would be wearing a civilian suit. I mean, he IS the Interim Prime Minister. In fact he was a pretty nice guy when I was introduced to him.

Bainimarama has a unique connection to the MFO. He served with the Force, but not as a member of the Fijian Infantry Regiment. He was a naval officer loaned out to the Italians. He served on board one of their patrol ships, the only non-Italian to ever do so, to my knowledge. Prior to that he attended a U.S. Coast Guard Search and Rescue course.

Things finally slowed down in December. Even though the security posture was slowly moving from "Beirut" to "Sarajevo" we managed to have a little fun. To raise money for a Black-And-White Party we did a traditional Army pie auction. These events saw soldiers bidding on the opportunity to throw a cream pie in the face of an officer or NCO... the higher the rank usually the more money to be raised. Claude splattered me with a pie for $80. That could have been some sort of revenge for my Felix Unger imitation that I do in our shared kitchen. I guess I'm not an easy person to live with.

I actually relaxed enough watch a football game... Manchester versus Liverpool. Manchester won in the first game I had watched in quite a while. Meanwhile, Tel Aviv was added to the areas off-limits to U.S. personnel. The camp's Israeli-supplied electricity was going out every once in a while. It was obvious that something is up.

I went with the Force Commander, the Force Sergeant Major and their wives on an aerial tour of remote sites in order to distribute presents to the Fijian, Colombian and American soldiers on duty there.

It was the first time that I had flown in a UH60 since leaving Iraq. The weather was pretty cold in the morning but it warmed up a little in the afternoon. In Iraq it seemed like it was ALWAYS hot.

My job was to take pictures while the party greeted the soldiers. There were a couple of funny things that happened during the trip.

At a Colombian site General Ludvigsen gave a short speech... while out of his sight the outpost's mascot (a HUGE dog) kept shaking his head as if he disagreed with everything the Force Commander said. At a Fijian site the Canadian sergeant dressed as Santa Claus looked on in horror as the biggest Fijian I ever saw sat on his lap. "Ho, ho, ho! What would you like... GET HIM OFF! GET HIM OFF! I can't feel my legs!!!"

149

## LOCAL TRANSPORT

Another incident was not so funny. At another Fijian site a motorcycle with two riders rolled up near the gate. They dismounted and the driver pretended to fiddle with the engine... except that the engine had been working fine before they stopped and he never actually used any tools on it. The second rider stared at us, emanating hostility as we walked from the helipad to the gate.

I wasn't the only one who sensed something was wrong. The FIJIBATT Commander, who was also on-site, made sure he was between the Force Commander and the two strangers as we entered. I informed some of our security people about the incident later and was told that such activities are no longer that unusual.

The next day Colonel Gerard went and did the Sinai Santa run. When he returned he told us at staff call that while the UH60 was aloft high enough to look beyond Zone Delta they could see Israeli F-16s lining up for attack runs on Hamastan. Gaza was being pounded in retaliation for mortar and Qassam rocket attacks on Israeli civilians. Peace talks between Israel and the Palestinian Authority had ended just last month but you wouldn't know it from where we were sitting.

The Sinai's rainy season began. In areas where you don't normally get rain a little bit makes a big difference. Some areas are quagmires and others have shallow pools which must be avoided. Oh, and the temperature suddenly plummeted.

Our Big Voice towers are still lying on the ground. As the rain falls. These tall towers are capped by what looks like a stack of flying saucers. They're designed to give audio warning and instructions in the event of an emergency. Unfortunately, a 100-foot crane is needed to lift them into place. So the project was put to bid and the lowest bidder got the contract. Unfortunately, the lowest bidder doesn't HAVE a 100-foot crane, he has a 75-foot crane.

From my understanding, the local business owner who got the contract then tried to "borrow" or hire a 100-foot crane from ANOTHER business. The other construction firms in our area are the same ones who lost out on the bidding to this Ali Baba, so naturally they aren't inclined to assist Ali in collecting the money for the contract.

It was weeks before a crane was procured, the towers lifted into place and the project was complete. Then it turned out that the MFO operations center didn't know how to operate the damn thing. The new tower next to my SOPV trailer was sending out random blasts of noise or conversation as the guys tried to sort them out, making it hard to concentrate on business.

We had a problem at the border at Nizzana. One of our runs into Tel Aviv was turned back. According to the Egyptians it was due to some of the

151

## BIG VOICE

Bedouins seizing the crossing and trying to "influence" the local authorities to release one of their own from jail.

I'd see the Bedouins near the fence when running, tending their flocks or just looking at our camp from a distance. The Bedouin are definitely different from their Arab brethren in El Arish and Sharm. They live in an extremely harsh environment and have their own laws for living their lives, independent of the Egyptian government.

Some of the Bedouin are not even descended from Arabs, at least not entirely. The ancestors of the Gebiliya Tribe originally came from the Balkans, either to build Saint Catherine's Monastery or to guard it. In any case, they stayed in the Sinai and had to learn to adapt to its harsh conditions. Now they are indistinguishable from the other tribes in the Sinai, at least to outsiders.

I never liked the way the Nile River Valley Egyptians looked down on the Bedo. Once, while I was on a flight back to the Sinai I sat next an Egyptian officer who spoke very good English. He started talking about the Bedouin.

"They are very ignorant and stupid people." He told me. "They are like those people you have who live in Kentucky and West Virginia in the mountains with their guns and liquor."

I felt my ire go up just a little but that was probably only because my great-great-great grandfather was captured in his home state of Kentucky while defending it from rebels. Or it might have had something to do with Great-Granpa running moonshine over from West Virginia during Prohibition. "You mean…. *Hillbillies*?" I asked, carefully enunciating the word.

"Yes!" he became very animated. "They are ignorant like hillbilly!"

I don't think I said much to him after that. I must not have or else I'm sure someone would have let me know.

There was great friction between the Bedouins and the Egyptian government. Until only a few years before, or so I was told, Bedouin were forbidden from getting driver's licenses. This placed them in a bad position as any police officer who could pull them over and they would have to pay *baksheesh* if they wanted to stay out of jail. Jail, even for a short time, was considered a horrible punishment to the Bedo, who have much more appropriate punishments available to deal with transgressions.

The Egyptian government seized beachfront property in the south in order to build the Red Sea resorts. Even though some Bedouin in the area sustained themselves with fishing no compensation (especially in the way of jobs) was offered. In al-Arish a museum was to be built highlighting the culture and history of the Bedouins… but the money somehow never got spent on that project.

I was told that part of the reason that the Bedouin are so badly treated by the national government is that during the Israeli occupation of the Sinai they were allowed to look after their own affairs without interference from Tel Aviv. In fact, the Israelis would provide some medical treatment for Bedos who arrived at their settlements in need of aid.

The Egyptian government saw this period of occupation as an opportunity for the Bedouin to mount guerrilla warfare against the Israelis. The Bedo failed to do this, probably because the Egyptian government by and large had little use for them up to and until they wound up behind "enemy" lines. So, when the Nile Valley Egyptians returned they treated the locals as collaborators.

The MFO's relationship with the Bedouin is much better. We would hand out bottles of water as a gift to the desert dwellers when one of our vehicles passed by, a small thing under any other circumstances but greatly appreciated in this part of the world. We had dinners with the locals. And frequently we would invite them to sell their crafts on North Camp. At the Bedo Market I bought a few trinkets. It's amazing how you see the same Chinese junk at these places, whether it's the Bedo Market in the Sinai, a flea market in Kentucky or the *flohmarkt* in Frankfurt a.m.: remote controlled toys, flip flops, talking mounted fish, etc.

# HOLE IN THE WALL

**12**

I Spent Christmas Day watching some videos by myself, including Santa Claus versus the Martians. Then the rumbling started, rattling windows and shaking doors. No one seemed to know if the explosions were coming from Gaza or the nearby Israeli artillery range.

We had a good Christmas dinner. Even if we couldn't be with our family and friends at least we could be with our comrades, with the new friends we made in the desert.

My crew spent the next few days finishing the Sandpaper. We had a lot of good photos but few graphics. In the meantime, the activity in Israel increased, mostly troop movements. A few Palestinians who were returning to Gaza from the Hajj were detained in Rafha... it seems they're known Hamas community organizers, i.e. terrorists.

We passed into 2008 and had a lot to look forward to. U.S. Representative Steve Israel (3rd District, NY) stopped by on a fact-finding tour. Another Bilat was announced for January 8th. The Hungarians were sending an An-26 resupply flight in. And just when I was trying to sort out those three visits my phone rang.

"Hello." a voice on the other end of the phone said. "I'm with the Air Force One Advance Team."

"Somehow, I had a premonition it would be you." I replied.

It turned out that President George W. Bush would be visiting Sharm el-Sheikh in the middle of the month as part of a Middle East peace tour. The advance team was looking for some security assistance from the USBATT during the visit but Colonel Gerard really wasn't in a position to support.

We thought that perhaps the advance party might require the use of our EOD team. This unit was originally assigned to help with all the leftover bombs and mines and other munitions from most recent three conflicts in the Sinai, but in a pinch they could deal with your typical terrorist device. However, the advon told us they weren't needed.

Meanwhile, I had a new problem... the Public Affairs Branch had not designated a replacement for me and my one-year tour was rapidly coming to an end. And yet, I had no orders in the works because I had no replacement. I was caught in another one of those Catch-22s made worse by the fact that I was

## THE WALL BLOWN UP

so busy that I had no time to deal with Branch. But I knew I didn't want to leave the next guy with the same situation I found myself in: arriving to fill a chair that had been empty for several weeks and figuring out everything worked on your own.

I went on the bus run to South Camp, just in case we had to assist with a visit of U.S. peacekeepers there. A long but uneventful trip, but when we got to South Camp we were told that there was absolutely NO plan for President Bush to visit U.S. peacekeepers. There was no time. It was out of his way. His security detail advised against it.

So what did we do? We got ready ANYWAY, just on the off chance that the Commander-In-Chief had an opening suddenly pop up on his calendar, an unexpected detour rerouted him by our gate, and his security detail changed their mind. I and other special staff types were on "standby," sitting around looking at each other in the USBATT HQ. Nothing came of it and I wasn't really surprised. It's too bad. I was hoping to demonstrate the new x-ray machine for the president.

We had been waiting for something to happen and it finally did. I was walking back to my house on January 22nd, 2008 when I heard and felt an explosion. If you've never been at war or routinely worked with artillery you might know explosions in the distance have a kind of gentle shock (or not so gentle!) that goes with them, something you never feel when dealing with, let's say, thunder. It was stronger than the explosions we had been hearing over the last few weeks. It also noticeably rattled the windows.

It turned out that Hamas had blown open a hole in the Gaza wall facing Rafah. People began crossing over at the hole and swarmed over the town of Rafah like a swarm of locusts. They began cleaning out the stores in town and when there was little left to purchase they moved on to al-Arish. A total blockade of the strip was declared by Israel but revoked not long afterwards... so long as the hole was there it was meaningless.

Initially the Egyptian border guards did nothing since they knew how Hamas propaganda had been whipping up the residents of Gaza against Egyptians. The Border Guard Force finally took steps to reassert control, laying down barbed wire to impede people from crossing, the mob attacked the BGF. We received a report that one border guard had is eyes gouged out. I hoped that wasn't true but I wouldn't be surprised considering Hamas's propaganda campaign.

The mainstream media portrayed the Palestinians crossing over from Hamastan as desperate, starving people. They made it sound as if they had swamped el-Arish and Rafah looking for food but that was not the case. I told some of my friends that I almost *wished* that CNN or Fox would call and ask me about conditions in the area so I could tell them "It's awful... you can't buy a pack of cigarettes for fifty miles around!"

Palestinians made more holes in the wall and created a vehicle crossing. Hamas then proposed that there be a joint control between itself Egyptian authorities. Knowing that such a deal would undermine their legitimate authority, the Egyptians did not even discuss the matter with Hamas.

There were a lot of proposals and counter-proposals being floated around the international community regarding Gaza's status. One was that Gaza should simply be administered by the Egyptians... which in fact it had been for many years during the second half of the 20th century. My personal feeling was that the Egyptians wanted nothing to do with this idea, even it was seriously bandied about... their occasional experiences thus far with Hamas did not leave them with the desire to repeat contact on a daily basis.

There was also a rumor that Israel might arrange transport for Palestinian Authority security forces from the West Bank to an Israeli-controlled crossing, where they would proceed to root out Hamas in Gaza. That idea seemed even less likely than returning Gaza to Egyptian administration. The Palestinian Authority didn't seem to have the stomach for dealing with the same kind of terror they had been dishing out for decades.

The Egyptians caught Palestinians on the border, apparently with the intent of blowing up targets in Sinai resort towns. How are hotels a legitimate military target? I guess it doesn't matter whether it's legit or not when you're dealing with terrorists.

About ten days later the Egyptian border guards moved in and resealed the breaches with surprisingly little bloodshed. In response, Hamas demanded SOLE control over the border crossing, no more talk of setting up a "joint" commission. They want that de facto recognition from the Egyptian government.

It seems clear to everyone that this will not be the end of it, even as the Israelis warns its citizens to prepare "rocket rooms" in case of renewed attacks. At about this time everyone was talking about the two suicide bombers who hit a mall in Dimona, Israel. One innocent killed and almost forty injured. The rumor was that the bomber had come from the Sinai, which later turned out to be untrue.

Task Force Sinai didn't let something as mundane as a nearby international incident get in the way of Army requirements. Suicide prevention classes and updated anthrax shots were the order of the day. Our suicide prevention classes are taught in such a way that, if you hadn't thought about

# CONSTRUCTION SITE

offing yourself before you might think about it at some point during the long, predictable course of the "training."

Once the official requirements were done, next was the Superbowl. Because of the time difference, people had to stay up until 0200 if they wanted to watch the game. I had about as much interest in watching the Superbowl as the Hungarians; all it meant for me was some extra sleep when work call was delayed that morning.

I was given the mission to pick up the Director-General at Qantara in the Canal Zone. We were delayed while they found an escort for us, a cargo van driven by two of the Uruguayans. With the SUV in the lead we headed out towards al-Arish. While we drove through it seemed a little crowded but otherwise not too crazy, considering stories of rock attacks against the local police and riots at nearby internment camps.

We were a little on edge initially but once we got clear of al-Arish and had nothing but tiny villages between us and the Suez Canal I relaxed a little bit. I was still fretting about my orders concerning the pick-up, or lack of them, when my Canadian driver perked up. "Hey, what's going on there?"

I looked to the opposite side, where the two eastward-bound lanes were. Egyptian Army trucks were rolling towards Israel. These were not open trucks but through side windows I could see someone, presumably soldiers, riding in the back.

"Treaty violation" was the first though to enter my mind. I grabbed the mike on the Motorola radio and tried to raise North Camp in order to place a report. I found that I was already out of range, out of range of any OP too.

This put us in a bind... did we continue to Qantara to get the DG? Or did we try to turn around and drive east until we came into radio range of the MFO? Keep in mind that the Egyptian trucks already pretty much OWNED that lane of the road. In practical terms, there seemed to be nothing to do but push on to the Suez Canal. We couldn't keep the Director-General waiting.

I counted vehicles for the report I would provide once we got back within radio range. The Egyptians were moving convoys and we saw fifteen trucks in the first group, thirteen in the second and six in the third. At least two companies of infantry, maybe more depending on how tightly packed the men were on those trucks. And all headed towards the Israeli border.

We arrived at Qantara to find the Director-General at the restaurant with the driver who brought him in from Cairo. On seeing us the driver departed and I reported to the DG what I just saw.

He took it very well. He didn't seem terribly concerned. Larocco got in the vehicle and we headed east to see for ourselves what was happening.

EGYPTIANS MOVE IN FORCE

An Australian instructor explains a HUMMVW to a U.S. Soldier. The Australians perform many staff and training functions within the MFO and have a well-earned reputation for toughness.

We passed no other vehicles headed towards the border. In fact, the drive was pretty boring… until we reached al-Arish. We were lucky to have left North Camp when we did, because if we had been delayed we might have run right into the Egyptian Army rounding up Palestinians when we drove through earlier. As it was, the Egyptians were still quite active in collecting the Palestinians (presumably to send them back to their side of the border) and from the occasional gunfire it seemed that a few were resisting. Egyptian soldiers were moving double-time in the streets with weapons ready. Once they were herded together Palestinians were loaded onto trucks.

I was extremely grateful that our van was well-marked as a peacekeeping vehicle. Our progress was reduced to a crawl as we navigated the street activity. I looked back to see how the DG was doing but he seemed to be working on his laptop. I couldn't tell if he was writing up a letter of protest to send to Cairo later or just playing solitaire.

Suddenly an Egyptian lieutenant colonel stepped in front of us. Without saying a word he pointed at the driver, then pointed to a street on our right. I nodded and told the driver "Do it." Pulled out my map to make sure we didn't get lost and finally called in a report.

It seemed that the Palestinians had overstayed their welcome and were now making a nuisance of themselves. Part of the reason the Egyptians were keen to evict them was the fact that the spending spree that the Gazans had been on was being paid for with counterfeit Egyptian pounds. So I guess they just don't fake American money, they do other people's too.

Another incident at Cairo International. A commo team from 1st TSC was supposed to be on its way to North Camp to install upgrades to our radio equipment and improve our communications. Unfortunately they arrived two weeks after they said they would come, which is not quite as bad as showing up two weeks BEFORE you have permission to come but it can still send the Egyptians into a tizzy.

This was bad enough but it got worse when the team's equipment was inspected and found to include a processor specifically prohibited for export under U.S. law. It seemed that this particular piece of equipment requires an end-user certificate by the U.S. Department of Commerce whenever it appears outside the United States. The Egyptians noticed this discrepancy and impounded the item.

Colonel Barnett has half the staff trying to figure out how to get this thing back on a plane and into North Camp. And somehow it was implied that it was SOPV's fault for not knowing this was going to happen.

How was I supposed to know that Claude and his Signal guys were going to fly in some high-tech gadget to fix the phones? How was I to know they were

FORTUNE AND GLORY

going to be dressed in civvies? How was I to know they would put the high-speed, nuclear-weapon grade processor in their luggage? Eventually it all got fixed but I felt justifiably annoyed.

Next I started working with the staff on a contingency plan for what to do if the CASA is no longer available. Primarily we were concerned with transport for the Egyptian bigwigs should they have to come out to the border for consultations. I'm not entirely sure WHAT we thought was going to happen to the CASA or WHY, and this was disconcerting given the mysterious crash of the Twin Otter.

In February we had the annual meeting of the Joint Military Cooperation Committee. This meeting saw the senior officers of Egypt's LAWIO and Israel's IDFSD meeting together to discuss long-term issues of interest to both parties. I had to provide three different briefings to the JMCC, reflecting the different hats I wore in the Sinai. This went well, although I was rushed to get them done in order to get the process back on schedule. In the meantime my crew kept the Officer's Club (the venue for the meeting) stocked with tea, coffee and other amenities.

Career-wise I seemed to be in limbo. No public affairs officer can be found to fill my slot, thus freeing me for departure. In any case, the leadership is inclined to keep me in the Sinai a bit longer, since I actually know how to do the job, especially with a visit from the U.S. Embassy Cairo in the works. I clearly have more than enough to keep me busy right up until the day I depart for good.

Towards the goal of getting out of Sinai SOMEDAY I did find time to get my Battle Handover Book done. This is basically a binder that has the job description, the schedule, the contacts, etc. needed to do the job position.

I also worked hard to close out all the requirements I had for the job, for instance making sure my NCOs were taken care of. Selmek had an NCO Evaluation Report due, which is very important when it comes to promotions and other personnel actions, and Jim asked if I could produce a letter of commendation, which would go into his Republic of Fiji Armed Forces record. I was glad to do this, as Jim was an enormous help during my time in the Sinai. I think I did a pretty good job on Selmek as well.

Branch wanted me to stay until my replacement got here. They had identified someone for the SOPV slot but couldn't tell me exactly when they would come.

At first I was willing to stay but later several things made me change my mind. First of all, it was the meetings. It seemed like we had meetings all the time, often with little value to the work I did. We had American meetings to

FINAL SHOPPING TRIP

determine how the U.S. Army staff would act during the Force meetings. We had meetings to determine how other meetings would go.

Then there was the fact that I wasn't getting properly recognized for the level of responsibility that I had assumed since arriving, dealing with diplomats, heads of state, senior military officials, etc. And finally, the whole incident with the Army Times made me feel like I was only good for doing the magazine.

I guess that the bottom line was that I felt I wasn't appreciated, even though I dealt with things on a daily basis that most other people wouldn't want anything to do with and even though I clearly knew the job. I always felt that I was not taken as seriously as other staff officers even though my job just as often had me traveling or working late or missing out on what few opportunities there were to relax in the Sinai. I told Branch to get my orders cut.

It didn't take long to get out-processed... after all, it wasn't like I had unaccompanied baggage to get picked up. There was a bit of going-away ceremony the day before I got on the bus to head back to Tel Aviv.

The trip was slow, a lot of time spent at the border. Both the Israelis and the Egyptians seemed a bit antsy over the situation with Gaza, especially since more rockets were being fired from the sometimes-safe haven of Hamastan. We weren't stopping at Be'ersheva anymore, which might have been due to a concern that the city might be within range of newer rockets fired from Gaza.

I arrived in Tel Aviv and checked into the hotel. I was worn out from weeks and weeks of what felt like nonstop work. But I felt good. I felt like I had accomplished something as a peacekeeper, and that despite the current troubles everything would work out fine. A long flight to Atlanta and a shorter one to Fayetteville and I would be done.

In the years since I left the Sinai things have gotten a bit crazy over there. Mubarak was forced to resign in 2011. His successor, Mohamed Morsi, was overthrown in a coup in 2013. In between, North Camp was overrun by "armed militants" who didn't actually kill anyone but there have been several deadly attacks against Egyptian forces in the Sinai.

In 2014 an ISIS affiliate calling itself the Sinai Province of the Islamic State announced itself by launching rockets into Israel... but from the Egyptian side of the shared border.

In January 2015 the Egyptian government began demolishing the town of Rafah. With no place to hide the entrances on the Egyptian side, Hamas will find it almost impossible to smuggle weapons and fighters to sympathizers in Sinai. Possibly in response, a rocket attack was launched against the North Camp airfield in June.

In September four American and two Fijian peacekeepers were injured by a roadside IED. In October 2015 a Russian airliner crashed, apparently brought down by a bomb. ISIS took credit for it.

On November 6th, 2015 the MFO announced that it had evacuated Checkpoint 1-F due to "an inability to safely resupply the site and continue conduct of its mission from that location." CP 1-F is only a few miles from North Camp. To my knowledge, it is the first time the MFO has ever had to abandon a post in the Sinai. Later, other sites were abandoned and FIJIBATT reduced its personnel.

Supposedly, a significant number of the MFO personnel at North Camp have been relocated to South Camp this year, in a move to reduce the danger from terror attacks.

The Multinational Force and Observers has been in the Sinai ever since 1982, but while the MFO's commitment to peace is as strong as ever, those who want violence, death and mayhem are just as determined to have war. Obviously ISIS will try to undermine the MFO just as Hezbollah undermined UNIFIL. Only time will tell which side will win in the Sinai: the side of peace and civilization or the side of chaos and barbarism.

# MISSING

## 13

I am putting out a world-wide alert for a missing wooden crate, picked up in early 2007 and supposedly shipped to North Camp in the Sinai via Tel Aviv, Israel. This crate is marked with the name "Major James D. Crabtree." It may have been sighted in Cologne, Germany. It contains U.S. Army uniforms, several books which were meant to improve my mind during my monastic existence in the desert (including a book called "Where's bin Laden?"), some art supplies, a brand-new camera lens that I never even got a chance to use, various references on public relations, and a sketchbook I had with me while I was in Iraq in 2005. At the very least the sketchbook has my name and contact information written on the inside cover.

This crate may be in storage somewhere or it might be simply have been shunted off to the side and forgotten in some corner of some airport or dock. It may even have been broken open and the contents auctioned off. In any case, I am extremely interested in recovering some or all of the contents. Especially the book about bin Laden.

Information should be sent to Doc Crabtree in care of this publisher.

I suspect President Mubarak knows where my crate is but he's not talking.

# GLOSSARY OF TERMS USED

1SB- 1<sup>st</sup> Support Battalion, a unit of the U.S. Army which provides the logistical support for Force operations. These were formerly provided by the LSU.

ADVON- An advance party arriving ahead of the rest of unit so billeting and other administrative matters can be sorted out.

AUSCON- Australian Contingent. Original service, 1982-1986 when it jointly manned the Rotary Wing Aviation Unit with the NZCON. In 1993 AUSCON rejoined the Force, providing administrative personnel and staff officers.

AVCO- Aviation Company. This combines the Rotary Wing and Fixed Wing functions. Aircraft consists of U.S. Army UH-60 helicopters and one C-12 Huron.

BILAT- A meeting held between members of two concerned parties; these meetings can be between the MFO and Egypt, the MFO and Israel, the MFO and the U.S. or between Israeli and Egyptian military leaders, in order to discuss issues of interest to both parties.

BRITCON- UK Contingent. Provided a headquarters unit from 1982 to 1995. In 2014 the UK "temporarily" rejoined the MFO in the form of a single staff engineer.

CANCON- Canadian Contingent. Canada joined the MFO in 1985, providing support to the RWAU. The Canadian Contingent divested itself of operating and maintaining the Force helicopters and now man the FFU and provides various staff officers.

COLBATT- Colombian Battalion, responsible for providing observation along the sector allocated to Colombian peacekeepers. Colombians also provide perimeter security for the camp itself.

Contingent- The unit, or group of units, belonging to a single nation and commanded by a single officer.

COU- Civilian Observer Unit.

CPU- Coastal Patrol Unit, provided by naval personnel of the ITCON and four patrol ships.

CZECHCON- Czech Contingent. The Czech Republic joined the MFO in 2009, providing staff officers, aircrew and an aircraft for the AVCO.

Director-General- The civilian chief of the MFO organization.

DUTCHCON- Dutch Contingent, part of the Force from 1982-1995. The Royal Netherlands Army filled the role of FMPU and also a small signals detachment. FC- Force Commander.

FEO- Force Engineer Officer. Oversees the construction and maintenance of camps and remote sites.

FFU- Flight Following Unit (Air Traffic Control). This is currently run by the Canadian Contingent.

FIJIBATT- Fijian Battalion, responsible for providing observation along the sector allocated to Fijian peacekeepers. Fiji also provides the Force Band and various garrison support personnel.

FMMC-

FMPU- Force Military Police Unit. This was initially provided by the Netherlands but the Hungarian Contingent assumed this role in 1995. Canadian peacekeepers took over this mission in 2015, when Hungary withdrew its contingent.

FPM- Force Provost Marshal. The MFO's chief law enforcement officer.

FRENCHCON- French Contingent. Provided the aircraft, aircrew and support personnel for the FWAU from 1982 to 2010, now provides some staff officers.

FSGU- Force Signals Unit. This unit provided internal and external communications and was manned by DUTCHCON until its withdrawal; functions were taken over by the LSU.

FSM- the Force's highest-ranking non-commissioned officer.

FWAU- Fixed Wing Aviation Unit. This unit provided air transport between the camps and was manned by the French Air Force. For a time this support was provided by DH-4 Twin Otter aircraft and later by a single CASA.

HUNCON- Hungarian Contingent. Hungary provided peacekeepers from 1995 to 2015 and filled the role of FMPU.

ITCON- Italian Contingent. The Italian Navy provides the Force's observation of the Gulf of Aqaba. See CPU.

LSU- Logistical Support Unit (see 1SB).

MFO- Multinational Force and Observers.

NORCON- Norwegian Contingent. Provides staff officers.

NZCMFO- New Zealand Contingent. Jointly manned the RWAU with AUSCON from 1982 to 1986; now providing training staff.

OCONUS- Outside the Continental United States, i.e. overseas service.

OP- Observation Post.

Peacekeeper- the general term used to describe members of the Force, regardless of nationality or role.

RWAU- Rotary Wing Aviation Unit, providing helicopter support to the MFO. This was initially in the form of UH-1 helicopters manned by Australian, New Zealander and Canadian peacekeepers. Later the United States replaced these with UH-60 Blackhawks and manned them with Army aviators.

SOPV- Staff Officer for Press and Visits.

TREU- Transport and Engineering Unit; provided by the Uruguayan Contingent.

TRILAT- an annual meeting hosted by the MFO and with representatives of Israel, Egypt and the United States. During trilats the Director-General reports to the three funds-contributing parties regarding the previous year's activities and future plans.

USBATT- U.S. Battalion, responsible for providing observation along the sector allocated to U.S. Army peacekeepers.

A. DIRECTOR-GENERAL'S AWARD. While the other two decorations are service medals, the Director Generals Award is based on merit. It is presented by the Director-General and nominees can be awarded to MFO or non-MFO members. The recipient is required to have made an extraordinary contribution to the Force mission or have exceeded goals set by the MFO. In the past outstanding leadership and professionalism have been recognized by the Director-General's Award, but individual achievements in innovation and services have also been recognized by the decoration. Ribbon colors are Orange-White-Green-Orange.

B. MULTINATIONAL FORCE AND OBSERVERS MEDAL. This decoration is awarded to all peacekeepers who serve in the Sinai for at least 6 months. It was established in 1982 and is the oldest of the MFO decorations. This is the medal awarded to all contingents and is usually presented at the end of rotation Medal Parades. Technically a one-time award, subsequent 6-month periods of service are indicated by a numeral device on the ribbon ("2" being the most common, recognizing a full year of duty in the Sinai). These are also presented at Medal Parades. Ribbon colors are Orange-Green-White.

C. MFO CIVILIAN SERVICE MEDAL. The CSM is a one-time award presented to civilians who serve the MFO in an honorable capacity. The medal itself is virtually identical to the MFO Medal but with a different ribbon. 360 days in the Sinai are required to earn the Civilian Service Medal but, unlike the Multinational Force and Observers Medal, numerals are not authorized for subsequent periods of service. Ribbon colors are Orange-Green-White.

OBVERSE

REVERSE

175

## ABOUT THE AUTHOR

James "Doc" Crabtree began his Army career in 1982 as a Hawk surface-to-air missile crewman and was later retrained to take his place in one of the first Patriot units then being formed. He applied to go to West Point Preparatory School (which was lost) and later applied for an Active-Duty ROTC Scholarship (which arrived AFTER he left the Army after his enlistment).

Crabtree was commissioned in 1989 and was placed back on active duty just in time for Operation Desert Shield in Saudi Arabia. He served as a Tactical Control Officer for a Hawk battery and operated a secret weapon attached to the Hawk called "Alpha." All efforts to get Hughes Aircraft to admit they built this thing (it had their name stamped on the components) have been fruitless.

When Desert Storm concluded Crabtree found himself in southern Iraq.

Following Gulf War I Doc Crabtree went to Ohio to get a graduate degree in history and worked for a time at the U.S. Air Force Museum. During this period he wrote *On Air Defense* and *Guerilla Air Defense.* He was asked to return to active duty in 1998 just in time to take part in Operation Desert Fox, which gave him the opportunity to visit Kuwait for the first time. Within a year he was off again, this time back to Saudi Arabia as part of Operation Southern Watch.

In 2003 Crabtree became a Public Affairs Officer and found himself in Iraq in 2005. The only time he was ever shot at was while he was serving in the U.S. Army as a PAO.

Doc Crabtree's next overseas assignment was in the Sinai, where he saw signs of the security situation there spinning out of control. He next went to Guantanamo Bay, where his detachment took care the pitifully few reporters interested in going to the detention facility following the election of President Obama.

Throughout his Army career Doc Crabtree has enjoyed drawing cartoons and has written for Army publications. In addition to his first two books (one of which was found in bin Laden's "library" during the raid that killed him) Crabtree has published a book about his experiences in Desert Storm with the Hawk surface-to-air missile system and a second, secret weapon that his unit was equipped with.

Made in the USA
Lexington, KY
16 February 2018